The departure point for inspiration is the obstacle.
Gianfranco Contini, *Varianti*

I enjoy having written, past tense.
Dan Brown

David Quantick really has written everything. As a television writer, he has written for *The Thick of It*, *The Day Today*, *Brass Eye*, *TV Burp* and many other shows. He is also an award-winning writer on HBO's *Veep* and wrote the critically praised Sky Arts *Playhouse*, *Snodgrass*. As a radio writer, he created Radio 4's *One* and Radio 2's *The Blagger's Guide*. His novel *Sparks* was described as 'excellent' by Neil Gaiman and his graphic series *Louis Wain* (created with Savage Pencil) was published in Alan Moore's *Dodgem Logic*. As well as a series of music books and the official biography of Eddie Izzard, David wrote the *Sunday Times* bestseller *Grumpy Old Men* and has written for over fifty magazines and newspapers, from the *Guardian* and the *Daily Telegraph* to *NME* and *Q*. With Jane Bussmann, he created the world's first internet sitcom, *The Junkies*. He is also the writer of several short films, including the highly acclaimed *Lot 13*. *How To Write Everything* is his first book about writing.

# DAVID QUANTICK

# HOW TO *write* EVERYTHING

OBERON BOOKS
LONDON

WWW.OBERONBOOKS.COM

First published in 2014 by Oberon Books Ltd
521 Caledonian Road, London N7 9RH
Tel: +44 (0) 20 7607 3637 / Fax: +44 (0) 20 7607 3629
e-mail: info@oberonbooks.com
www.oberonbooks.com

A catalogue record for this book is available from the British Library.

PB ISBN: 978-1-78319-103-1
E ISBN: 978-1-78319-602-9

Cover illustration by Steven Appleby

Chapter illustrations by James Illman

Printed and bound by Replika Press Pvt. Ltd., India.

# Contents

This book is dedicated to all the people who made me a writer, with particular thanks and gratitude to:

Malcolm Imrie

Neil Spencer

Geoffrey Deane

Jane Bussmann

Kate Haldane

and Steven Wells

# WITH THANKS TO

All the interviewees – Ben Aaronovitch, Joss Bennathan, Andrew Cartmel, Geoffrey Deane, Tanika Gupta, Michael Knowles and Dan O'Brien – for their time, knowledge and humour.

George Spender at Oberon for overseeing, encouragement and all-round excellence, Ian Greaves for bringing us together, and Kate Haldane for being the best agent since agents began.

Jenna Quantick for being lovely and for the quote about improv, Alexander Quantick for taking the mouse and keyboard from me whenever possible, my parents Mike and Sheila Quantick, and everybody I've ever read and learned from.

# Introduction

This book is called HOW TO WRITE EVERYTHING for two reasons. One, it sounds good. A phrase that sounds good is generally better than one that doesn't sound good. This is why academic texts are often awful. They're written by people who not only don't care that their work is unreadable, they quite possibly believe that being unreadable adds an extra layer of credibility, much like an improvisational musician believes that playing a twenty minute piece of music with no hooks or melody makes their work superior to a three minute pop song with verses and a chorus.

The second reason for calling this book HOW TO WRITE EVERYTHING is practical. Everything in this book is practical, starting with the title, which is practical because it is a precise description of the contents. This book will tell you how to write everything. Not anything, anyone can do that, even an academic or someone who thinks 'beryllium' is a sentence. This book is written by me, and I have written everything. I actually have.

Here, for the beryllium brigade, is a list of things I have written:

Sketch shows (and sketches)

Sitcoms (and sitcom pilots)

The world's first internet sitcom

Film scripts

Short film scripts

Non-fiction books (including a biography, rock books, comedy books, and this, by the time you read it)

Fiction books (three and a half unpublished novels, and one self-published but with comments from writers like Neil Gaiman and Ben Aaronovitch. Well, Neil Gaiman and Ben Aaronovitch. Favourable comments too.)

Radio shows

Television shows

Voice-over scripts

Award show scripts

Wedding speeches

Letters for friends

Poems (arguably)

Slogans for T-shirts, underpants and bags

And journalism, for over fifty magazines, newspapers and periodicals. (Sometimes just once. Here's a quote, for quote fans. The writer and journalist Frank Harris once boasted to Oscar Wilde that he had been invited into the homes of many famous people. 'Yes, Frank,' said Wilde. '*Once.*') I have written columns for national newspapers, reviews and interviews for music papers in the UK and the US, and I have even written for comics (I once wrote some storylines for *The Dandy*, which makes me very happy).

I present this list not to show off (it does rather illustrate what a hack I am) but because I'm always suspicious of books written by people who Haven't Had Anything Made. As a British TV writer, there are lots of things I Haven't Had Made, but I make this list as evidence that I have been there and done that (and on at least one occasion written the T-shirt). I've been to the meetings, had the rejections and the acceptances, endured the patronizing ('You've got it half right,' my writing partner and I were once told), waited for the cheque that never came and everything else that comes with the job. And I WILL REVEAL THE SECRETS OF WRITING. (Secret Number One: there are no secrets. Wait, come back...)

Oh, and although I have written everything, I haven't actually written everything in this book. Partly because it pays to delegate (e.g. take the credit for other people's work) but also because I didn't want this to be one of those books where somebody with no success in writing drama, poetry or limericks dished out advice to people about writing drama, poetry or limericks. With that in mind, my brilliant editor George Spender and I have approached various friends and acquaintances to, as it were, shade in the areas where ignorance is preponderant. Thus you will find that some parts of this book are me making statements and other parts are me asking questions. Everyone I've interviewed has had success and is experienced in their area of writing. We are belt and we are braces.

This book is also divided into handy chapters for quick reference, and each chapter covers one or more aspects of writing, from getting commissioned to getting ideas, from working with actors to working with yourself and many other topics. It contains useful anecdotes from my own career and stories I have been told (although sadly I could not shoehorn in the John Gielgud umbrella story. We'll see[1]).

One more thing. If you want – and you probably should want – the names and the addresses of everyone I've ever known, you won't find them here. For three reasons: one, the contact details of those who work in television, radio, publishing, film and so on change all the time, as people move a lot. Two, if you can't work

---

1    See Appendix: The John Gielgud umbrella story.

out for yourself how to track down someone who works for a company, you may not be suited to the rough and tumble of commercial writing. And three, I will instead give you valuable advice on how to deal with these people (see Chapter Six: Hunting Down and Killing Television Producers. Joking).

So thank you for getting this far. Don't steal this book, it took me ages to write, and besides, we're writers. We stick together.

## Chapter One
# What is Writing?

**H**ello.

And by writing that word, just one word, you are on the road to writing your first novel or screenplay or play or sketch show. Or so we are told. In fact, by writing the word 'hello', you are on your way to being someone who has written one word and that's it. That's all she wrote. The world is full of people who've written one word, or done this:

SCANDALOUS TUMBRILS: A Novel
by Sam Tenpole.

SCANDALOUS TUMBRILS by SAM
TENPOLE: A Novel

S. TENPOLE. SAMUEL K TENPOLE. SK
TENPOLE

A STUDY IN TUMBRILS: THE SECOND
SCANDALOUS TUMBRIL NOVEL
by Dame Sam Tenpole, FRCS

And the world is also full of people who stopped there. Because the first step on a journey is not the most important. They all are. Especially the middle steps, the 'I can't go on, Sarge, you and the lads go on without me' steps. The secret of writing is, oddly enough, writing. If you don't write anything, there won't be any words on the paper. Stephen King, in a book called *On Writing*, which is worth reading, said something to the effect that he's constantly meeting people who say they 'want to write', to which his mental reply is, 'No, you don't, because if you did, you would.'

Writing is very boring, except when it isn't. Writing takes, literally, time, which is why pulp writers and romance writers famously dictate their novels, because that's the fastest way to get the words out (and don't think for a moment that these writers are no good because they write so much they can't remember what they've written. When I interviewed P.D. James, probably our greatest crime writer, she quite happily admitted that she couldn't remember the names of most of her characters). Writing doesn't have to be the soul-ripping, heart-sucking process we are led to believe it can be. You can be a glib writer and be just as good as the writers who can only dribble out a word an hour. Conversely, the slow writer, the one who writes a paragraph a day, is no worse than the speedy columnist. It's words; you just have to get them down.

This is obvious advice, like most advice, but it's true. You have to do the writing. You can pay someone else to do it (you may even get paid to do someone else's writing) but someone has to write it. And the best way to do that is to stop fiddling about with the stuff on your desk and write.

A word on desks. I would advise you to forget all those idiot books about The Writer's Place of Work which show a lovely desk surrounded by knickknacks and images torn from magazines. You can write anywhere if you want. Dylan Thomas wrote in a boathouse. Roald Dahl wrote in a shed. Noël Coward and Ian Fleming wrote in a lovely house in Jamaica, but not at the same time. I've written on airplanes, in hotels and on more than one occasion I have written a newspaper column on my phone on a crowded train.

If you don't have a phone, use a pen. If you don't have a pen, use a pencil. And if you have nothing to write with, make like the man in the Borges story about the firing squad and compose your words in your head (seriously, if your idea is good, the memory is a brilliant place to repeatedly road test it).

'But I'm not inspired!' you say. 'The words will not come!' Actually, to paraphrase a saying from a film, if you write them they will come. When you're stuck, start writing. It may be, and almost certainly will be, awful, but if you have a vague idea of what you want (and sometimes even if you don't) a shape will form, an idea will loom out of the fog like a golem, and you'll have your starting point. I wrote a few pages like that recently. After a minute or two, I noticed the speaker (it was in the first person) talked like he'd been translated. I kept this style, decided he was a translator who'd become influenced by the way translators write, and I had the beginnings of a character.

There's another saying, I believe, about sculpture, that people carving a piece of stone aren't shaping it, they're releasing the sculpture inside it. I would have called this a piece of sculptor's tosh if I hadn't experienced exactly the same feeling when writing: sometime it feels like you've got a page and when you write on it, there's a story underneath, like a kind of prosey brass rubbing.

Jerry Seinfeld, the comic and writer, stunned a lot of people when he gave his advice to writers as 'write every day.' This is a spectacularly sane maxim; as Seinfeld points out, athletes exercise every day, and musicians practise every day. If you write every day you will get better. You may also be aware of the novelist's maxim (it's a page for maxims, this): you have to write a million words before you become a good writer. Not because it's a test, but because simply writing that much makes you better, just as lifting heavy weights every day makes you stronger. Writing isn't just a magic creative process; it's a form of exercise that also gives you the benefit of mental muscle memory.

The other great thing about writing to write, by the way, is that it's a great releaser. Just as nothing you read is ever wasted (I once wrote a Dylan Thomas parody based on the Keep Britain Tidy warning on a packet of crisps. It was a poem called 'Do Not Throw Me On The Ground When I Am Empty'), so nothing you write is pointless. It might turn out to be 500 words containing one great joke or one-liner. It might be the kernel of a poem. It might be a character in the wrong story who would be better as the central character of a novel. You never know. And if you sit around waiting for inspiration, you never will know.

The next chapter is the one about ideas, so I'll leave off that topic for now. But I will just drop in my all-time favourite theory. This is a theory I thought I'd invented until I came across it again in a Clive James book called *Cultural Amnesia*, where he attributes it to an Italian writer called Gianfranco Contini. (The book is massive but every page is a new idea, so read it.) And the theory (my version, anyway) goes something like this; when you have an obstacle to writing, incorporate the obstacle (Contini puts it a lot better, as you will of course recall from the quotation at the start of this book).

If you're writing a musical about life in Regency London but your cast are French and your orchestra can only play the banjo, then don't make them learn awful English or give them violins, find a reason for the characters to be French and for the music to be played on banjos. Perhaps it's now a musical about French nobility escaping the Revolution and then introducing the banjo to Louisiana. Perhaps it's something else (I would go with something else). Either way, use the problem, incorporate the flaw, and turn the obstacle into the selling point. As Contini put it, when life gives you lemons… I'm joking, he probably never said that. (He was actually referring to the fact that writing in rhyming verse, which obviously makes it harder to convey ideas or construct sentences, is in fact the key to better poetry.)

Of course, this is only my opinion, based on twenty-five years of writing comedy, journalism, fiction and for *The Dandy*. Others have equally valid views. There are, for example, people who believe writing to be a loose collection of brilliant words. By which I mean obscure words. Lists of things like archipelago, bellwether, cumbersome, diadem, ecky thump and so on. (Actually, 'ecky thump' is brilliant.) The most famous example of this, outside the pages of American novels, is a letter from the copywriter turned screenwriter Robert Pirosh, who wrote a job application letter where he went on at some length about the words he liked ('elegant, flowery words, such as estivate, peregrinate, Elysium, halcyon' – amazingly, he wasn't shot for this, and went on to write for the Marx Brothers). Maybe he and others are right, and writing is in fact an endless shopping list of otiose verbiage. But if you're going to write well, if you're going to write for anyone's fun but your own, if you're going to write anything – then I would suggest you ditch all that. Words are not archaic jewels to be strewn. They're the things you put in your sentences to give them meaning, not just effect.

The use of words, or 'word usements' as Jon Culshaw's George W. Bush used to put it, is something of a moot point because it does rather depend what, or where, you're writing. I once wrote a live review of Prince for the *Daily Mail* and, being sane, used the word 'Prince' whenever I wanted to refer to Prince. I hadn't realised, however, that one of the quirks of the *Mail* at the time was the journalistic, or specifically sub-editor's, practice of avoiding repetition at all costs (even in a 200 word review, where repetition is generally minimal unless you've gone mad and just write 'Prince Prince Prince Prince' over and over). As a result, the first time I wrote 'Prince', the sub-editor called him 'Prince'. The second time I wrote 'Prince', the sub changed 'Prince' to 'the diminutive pop star.' The third time I wrote 'Prince', the sub changed it to 'the miniature moppet'. Or similar. And so on. By the time the review ended, I believe Prince had been called every synonym for 'short house' available. The result, I maintain, was absurd, but it is a house style.

I should emphasise very strongly here that I am very much in favour of subs and production staff. From time to time you'll see a piece online by some nimrod complaining about how their deathless prose was tampered with by some ignorant sub. Subs are in fact rarely ignorant; they're experienced journalists who know how to make your work look right in the context of a newspaper or magazine. Some of my best friends, literally, are production staff, freelance editors and subs. They spend most of their time complaining about the illiterate writers whose work they have to correct, rewrite and generally make readable in every sense of the word. Do not disrespect them, do not patronize them and never mess with them, or else you will look like a monkey.

But back to house style. Every magazine, every TV show, every industry has one, from the extreme (Hollywood agents won't read a movie script if it's not printed on the right *size* of paper, never mind in the right format) to the brilliant (most of the really good writers I know started on the almost literally insane 1980s teen pop magazine *Smash Hits*, whose house style resembled a slightly drunk gay man in a very good if bitchy mood). If you want to be a journalist, or even a columnist, you should at the very least be aware of the house style of the mag or blog or thing you are writing for. I've written columns for the *Mirror*, the *Telegraph* and *The Times* and they all have their own style, partly based on their readership demographic and partly on practical factors like the amount of space you've got. Feel free to rebel against these strictures if you want to (i.e. be a ponce) but like all rebels, understand what you're rebelling against. Or just learn from a great writer, the novelist and columnist Keith Waterhouse, whose *Waterhouse on Newspaper Style* is without doubt the greatest book on writing I've ever read. Clear, funny, and definitive, *Waterhouse on Newspaper Style* is a book everyone should read, and I do mean everyone. (Brief aside: Keith Waterhouse's novels are masterpieces. You should read them, especially his two Billy Liar books, *Billy Liar* and *Billy Liar on the Moon*.)

Another thing you might want to know about writing: deadlines are good for you. Yes they are. I know you read that very funny quote by Douglas Adams: 'I love deadlines. I like the whooshing sound they make as they fly by.' And perhaps that quote has made you believe that deadlines are unimportant or worse, that they're a hindrance to, you know, the true creative process where ideas are like birds that alight a moment upon the windowsill of your computer and drip, I dunno, sort of creative honey into the mouth of your brain and then fly away to feed Martin Amis.

It probably does work that way for some writers who wait for the Muse to strike them, as though the Muse were a kind of mugger who lies in wait for the artistic sort and whacks them with a sock full of inspiration. But for most writers, in most fields, deadlines are useful. For a start, they're there for a reason. Deadlines are essentially time limits: they tell the writer when their content is needed for publication or recording. If you miss the deadline, you could be holding up a printer, a studio session, actors, editors, and so on. Perhaps that doesn't matter to you; perhaps your work is so fabulous that if it turns up after everyone else has given up hope, they'll still be delighted just to have it.

But deadlines are also a great starting pistol. Any writer (which in this case is nearly every writer) can tell you that a lot of time when you should be writing is in fact spent – all together now! – staring out of the window. Going online. Playing – ha ha! – computer games. Anything but actually writing. This has nothing whatsoever to do with 'writer's block' (possibly because, I maintain, there's no such thing as writer's block, if you're doing it properly). It is however a lot to do with 'I can't be bothered.' A lot of the time, writers simply don't feel like writing because what for? Who cares if you write anything? And even if you do surely it can wait? The world isn't going, 'I really hope someone writes a prequel to *Sense and Sensibility*' or 'Please hurry and write a buddy cop movie where one of the cops is actually a cat!' There's plenty enough to read and watch and listen to.

Which is where deadlines come in. Deadlines, like the hanging of English admirals in *Candide*, are there to encourage you, that is, to literally give you heart. Someone cares! Someone will pay you to write! And more importantly, someone cares and will you pay you to write if you do so RIGHT NOW. Or at least before Friday. So respect deadlines. They are incentives, they are engines, they are reasons. (And if you miss them, don't worry; editors generally lie about them to get you to deliver ahead of time.)

The practicalities of writing, there. I'm a big fan of productivity and time spent at the coal face and so on. But I only pride myself on being a hack to a certain, finite extent. There's nothing wrong with being a hack, in fact there's a lot right with it – the ability to work under pressure, the ability to function in a way like a mimic and produce a variety of different kinds of writing to order – and I'd like to take a moment to consider the most underrated aspect of writing – writing to order.

In an authored, authenticity-obsessed world, being able to disguise yourself as someone else is seen as somehow dishonest, fake even. Performers write their own material, singers write their own songs, and the idea of a skilled craftsperson producing work for others is considered wrong. Obviously this is drivel – no one thinks less of you if you haven't made your own furniture or built your own car – but scripted reality shows and karaoke-style pop acts haven't helped. (Weirdly, the most faker-hate is reserved for the entirely innocuous audience sitcom, because filming people laughing at jokes is wrong. Nonsense. Audience laughter, canned or not, is no worse or better than over-dubbing strings on a song. Now go and find an acoustic laptop.)

But most actors can barely speak, most presenters know their topic like the back of a stranger's hand, and even most comedians will use up a career's worth of material in the course of one television show. Writers don't always get to be the lead singer; more often, we're the session men, making The Monkees sound great. I could go on at great length about the absurdity of the authentic, but I won't (although you might be interested in what heritage record companies do with freshly digitised and sharpened photos of their long-dead blues acts. They age them, is what) so instead I'll take a moment to big up us writers who work Tirelessly Behind The Scenes.

As a white, male, middle-aged, middle-class comedy writer from Devon, I have written material for gay female stand-ups, working-class West Indian comics, Northern lads and upper-class boys. As a voice-over writer, I have explained the science of food and nutrition in script form for a not-necessarily science-based presenter to read out. As a wedding speech writer, I've written jokes about people I've never met. And I once wrote a script for Sir George Martin explaining how he had met The Beatles, which I'm sure he knew already. (I introduced myself to Sir George afterwards and explained the paradox that had connected us. He smiled and said, 'I'm terribly sorry, I'm afraid I'm very deaf.')

The ability to capture someone's voice is useful in a writer, whether it's a performer, a personality or even the house style of a magazine. (I remember my first

*NME* editor Neil Spencer subbing the gossip column and saying with a loud tut: 'We don't say 'I'.) How could it not be? Any fool who believes that to write a novel about a coal miner or a film about an unemployed nurse you have to be a coal miner or an unemployed nurse is, yeah, a fool. Because what if your film or book has another character in it, someone who isn't a miner or a nurse? Do you then retrain as a teacher or cruel landlord? And what about novels set in Roman times? Or science fiction films? Should the *Alien* movies have been written by aliens?

Writers should generally have a distinctive voice, but equally generally they should have other voices. Usually we do say 'I', but not always.

The practicalities there. Now let's take a moment to consider the impracticalities, as it were. The ineffable. Because I speak of course of the authorial voice. And also of the poetic voice. And individuality and difference in general. We are all, as Newton and Oasis put it, standing on the shoulders of giants, but some people seek to be the giants themselves. Others just want to do work which hasn't been done before. A few years ago, I thought of a sketch show format which to my knowledge was genuinely different. I emailed it to an independent radio producer and within weeks (a week being a very short time in radio) it had become a series. It was called *One*, and the format was that each sketch was an individual voice. (It differed, as I had to point out to pedants, from the work of monologuists like Alan Bennett and Joyce Grenfell in that we employed a variety of actors and scenarios, not just one performer playing different characters.)

Sometimes chance makes you creative. When the great Jane Bussmann and I decided to get around the problem of no sod wanting to make any of our ideas and film our own sitcom pilot, we first of all lit on the idea of creating a comedy about heroin addicts, called *The Junkies*, which was a first (fifteen years later, no other smackedy has yet been made). It was then suggested to us by our producer, Jess Search, that we should put it on a website and allow people to watch it on broadband, which had come in about two days before. We were then able to claim, with a slight degree of accuracy, that we had put up the world's first internet sitcom. (It's now on YouTube, sadly off a videotape.)

On occasion, though, to be creative you have to throw aside all pretence of efficiency and practicality and just – oh, I don't know, sit cross-legged in the middle of an ashram, whatever that is, and wait for the Muse to strike you. Or go for a long walk through the Black Forest. Or take a lot of LSD. Or any of the Tools of Creative Writers. You can even buy books about the *Tools of the Creative Writers*. They're not very useful; some writers get drunk, others must be sober. Some listen to music to inspire them, other can't have any outside stimuli at all. And so on.

Creativity can, as I have suggested, be forced simply by performing the act of writing until something happens. But sometimes it needs to be coaxed out, like the tapeworm in Vivian Stanshall's *Sir Henry At Rawlinson End*, with a pat of butter on the pillow or similar. And this topic will be dealt with more thoroughly in Chapter Two.

## Chapter Two
# Ideas and Where They Come From

O ne of the great clichés of the question-and-answer session at conventions and other events where writers sit on a stage and people who've bought their books, seen their films or just wanted their money back, come and see them is this: someone in the audience always puts their hand up and says, 'I've always wondered – where do you get your ideas from?'

Writers have a variety of responses to this, from the flippant (Neil Gaiman: 'From the Idea-of-the-Month Club') to the serious (Stephen King: 'My ideas come from making connections, and sometimes those connections are very sudden and to some degree beyond my conscious control'), but the first part of the real answer is this: it depends. Kingsley Amis once hailed a cab at the same time as a non-white man. The cab driver ignored the other man and stopped for Amis, who knew then he had an idea for a novel. I knew I had an idea for a series when I realised all the sketches I'd been writing were for one voice. Steve Coogan knew he had an idea for a film when he read *Philomena* by

Martin Sixsmith. Shakespeare knew he had an idea for a play about two star-crossed lovers when he saw a play about the story of *Romeo and Juliet*. Cole Porter based 'Miss Otis Regrets' on a visiting card. Paul McCartney wrote 'Picasso's Last Words' when Dustin Hoffman bet him he couldn't write a song 'about anything'.

And so on and so forth: an idea can come from anything at all. (It doesn't even have to be an idea; in the vexed thicket of improvisation, which we shall come to later, an idea may well form from what is often, frankly, a lot of waffle.)

What makes an idea a good idea? It's not an objective thing; a good idea is simply one which inspires something you are capable of writing, something that might sustain. When Kingsley Amis, again, went into the lecturers' common room at a provincial university, he realised nobody had written about that world before. Someone else might have got a slightly dull story about universities out of that, but Amis added to that some suggestions from his best friend Philip Larkin (and some aspects of Larkin's romantic life) and he created a new kind of post-war comic novel (*Lucky Jim*).

Your idea might be best written as a poem, a song, a sketch or even a Tweet (social media are a great home for the one-off remark) but it can be anything at all. It can be simple yet lead to an epic (books like *The Lord of the Rings* are massive yet not complex works, and movies like *Inception* are often just traditional stories hidden in geometric patterns) or it can be complicated and short (riddles and jokes are often like that).

And it doesn't have to be entirely complete. Philip Larkin (again) said something to the effect that writing a novel is like planning a long journey by car to Scotland; you know where you're going to set off from and where you want to end up, and there are a few landmarks along the way, but the rest is something you will fill in as you go. Larkin of course abandoned the novel for poetry (in which he showed astonishing control) and there are several authors who'd disagree (Graham Greene, like many other writers, planned his chapters meticulously) but his point is still valid; an idea doesn't have to be born with legs; like a tadpole, it can grow them later when it needs them.

What the idea is doesn't matter: it's an idea and even if it doesn't lead anywhere, it's still an idea and it proves that you can have ideas, and if you keep working at having ideas, you will have *better and better* ideas and eventually you will have *brilliant* ideas. Some very talented people don't have ideas, in any useful sense; this is why the world is full of brilliant musicians who've never composed an original song, songwriters who still have to rhyme 'moon' with 'June', poets who write greetings cards, and writers who can adapt novels and stories for television and cinema but have never come up with their own TV show or film. All of these people are skilled, entertaining and even inspired; but if you can generate your own material from start to finish, whether it's creating a film script or coming up with an angle for a magazine article, that's arguably much more rewarding.

I am in short hinting strongly that you already have ideas. Unless you've only ever been a writer, you will have some experience of the world and that will give you input. And not just that: even if you've never been in a relationship or suffered from unrequited love, even if you've never been in education or been home-schooled, even if you've spent your life in a cave with no books or internet, even if you've done nothing, you have your imagination. (Of course, if you have no imagination and just want to Write From Life, that's also entirely reasonable, but if that's the case you might want to get a job on a trawler or marry an axe murderer, just for the experience. But trust me, it's easier to make things up.)

Ideas are everywhere and can be anything; the trick is to identify them as ideas. And to identify them as dead ends. As a comedy writer, I often have people say to me, 'You could put that in a sketch', but generally I couldn't, for a variety of reasons. I've sort of implied that any idea is valid, but as I said above, an idea has to sustain; one way to spot a non-writer is their hoarding of the great idea they're going to get around to doing. Peter Cook said to me (in an interview, we weren't bowling buddies) that people were always telling him how funny their mate was and what a great comic he would be.

'Well,' said Cook, 'Why doesn't he do it then?' A fair point, and part of the answer is that having a couple of gags and the ability to make your pals laugh doesn't mean you can get onstage night after night, in front of people who don't know you and sustain an act and a career for years on end. Similarly, the person nestling an idea in their bosom may secretly know that their idea, if exposed to the light, will turn to dust, or look stupid in a way they can't deal with, or have been done, or just not work.

That's not to say an idea needs to be new to work. I've mentioned Shakespeare's penchant for adapting other people's plays and stories; it was a perfectly legitimate practice in days of old to rework a familiar theme, just as film studios today endlessly revisit the origin stories of *Batman* and *Spiderman*, and TV companies return again and again to Charles Dickens and Jane Austen. And that's just the brands: you must never be discouraged when someone says, 'But your idea is just XXX with a twist.' All stories are XXX with a twist; there are books about the archetypes – and they're worth reading, both to understand how stories work and to nick the stories therein. (This doesn't just apply to fiction; no journalist was ever discouraged by someone saying, 'But there's already *been* an article about Higgs-Boson.')

Look at a TV show like *Mrs Brown's Boys*. It's a huge hit in the UK and it cut a swathe through the schedules with its fresh take on comedy and a central character new to most viewers. But it is, in my informed opinion, utterly unoriginal. Many of the jokes are pub jokes, not generated by the show's writer, but remembered and transferred to television. The situation isn't original, the humour isn't original, and the premise is so vague as to be almost conceptless (a TV executive recently told a friend of mine, 'We don't want high concept. We want a familiar face with a supporting cast.') But it works, brilliantly. The central character is powerfully portrayed and is a cheeky clown. The jokes are thickly spread and constant. And the origin of the show is significant; it began as a novel, *The Mammy*, which became a film starring the Hollywood actress Anjelica Huston (who has a strong connection with Ireland), and spun out into a comparatively lukewarm Irish TV series and a stage show. The current version shown in the UK is the culmination of all those versions, but mostly it's a straightforward transfer of the stage show; with its addresses to the audience, constant fourth-wall breaking and bawdiness (not to mention a central character in drag), *Mrs Brown's Boys* is pure music-hall. It's not just unoriginal, it's a throwback to the olden days. And it works, because of all that.

So please don't bust a gut trying to be original. It may not be you. Some people work best by pushing the boundaries back as far as possible. Some people loathe cliché. Chris Morris, a serial avoider of anything that's been done before, once remarked to me of a fellow writer, 'He's still at the aardvark stage of comedy,' meaning someone who finds that kind of word hilarious and has not yet moved on from there. Harsh but funny. It's not a bad stance to take – and I for one long never to hear someone say to me, 'It's a sitcom set on A ROCK PAPER!' or 'It's about some people TRYING TO RUN A RADIO STATION!' – but it's not the only one. An idea is often just a conventional container for something more exciting. Look at *The Simpsons*, or *Modern Family*, both comedies about family life, neither of which embrace convention. Take *Green Wing*, set in the overdone world of hospitals, but unlike any other hospital show ever.

And if you have an original idea, be prepared to find yourself a prophet without honour or at the very least the Queen of the Idiots. I do not wish to add more fuel to the traditional writers' paranoia of 'Nobody understands my genius' (everybody understands your genius, they just don't want to work with somebody as arrogant as you) or 'I had that idea ten years ago' (so did everyone else) but the fact does remain, original ideas are always harder to sell than unoriginal ideas.

Here's an example. About ten years ago I was asked to write a book 'inspired by' a well-known television series. 'Inspired by' is an odd term, as it can just as easily mean 'uninspired by,' and is often a synonym for 'copied from.' In publishing there's the expression 'passing off', which is a very bad thing and means you have ripped someone else off. The book I was to write was inspired by the television series *Grumpy Old Men*, whose format consisted of men in early middle-age complaining about aspects of modern life. The publisher wanted to call the book '*Grumpy Old Men*.' I wanted to call it something less direct and replete with confusion, like the '*Grumpy Old Book*', so readers would know it was a bit like the series but not actually the series (you'll notice I didn't refuse the commission). The publishers felt that wasn't necessary, and the book I wrote was different enough to the series; it wasn't a set of interviews with middle-aged men, it was all by me, and the cover design (and the words 'inspired by the BBC series') meant it was, fairly clearly, not an official book.

As the BBC, with their usual attention to speed, had not at this point put out their own *Grumpy Old Men* book, ours did very well. (I am still not convinced that anyone bought it for themselves, or that any of the people who had it bought for them actually read it; it was a gift book, whose title and relevance to the recipient would be the joke on Father's Day, or Christmas Day, or Book To Keep In The Toilet Day.) There were two sequels, both of which did less well, partly because sequels do less well and partly because the BBC woke up and, quite understandably, flooded the market with official *Grumpy Old Men* books, *Grumpy Old Men* diaries, *Grumpy Old Women* books, *Grumpy Old Men on Holiday* books and so on.

The point of this story is that cashing in on someone else's success is a lot easier than doing all the work yourself. Why go through all the effort and poverty endured by J.K. Rowling to sell a new children's series when you can just wait for the *Harry Potter* brand to become huge and do your own child wizard novels (the names of which successors have all escaped me and any you think of are not copies of J.K. Rowling). Why not find a way to parody someone's work? Like we did in the wake of the success of *The Dangerous Book for Boys* and its ilk, although our *Dangerous Book for Middle-Aged Men* was not a success.

The high point of this process for me, by the way, was going to lunch with a publisher to discuss a way of following in the footsteps of the then newly popular *Is It Just Me or Is Everything Shit?* books. We spent an hour or so trying to think of phrases with the word 'shit' in them and got as far as *Shit Happens* before we abandoned the whole thing. It was probably a good idea. (Oh, and some years ago a comic I was working with asked the originator of the *Grumpy Old Men* TV series if he'd ever met me. 'I have not sought out the pleasure of his acquaintance,' he replied, brilliantly.)

So originality is not necessarily prized. This is because you are almost certainly writing for people who want a quick and certain profit as they don't wish to starve to death. The days of the BBC putting out entire series of sitcoms until finally, on series three, the show is a hit, are gone. Even Sky, who began their new comedy scheduling with a staggering run of fresh commissions, are slowing up (although, for a station whose viewers mostly tune in for sport and movies, they are loyal to the comedy shows they have). In magazines, you will find that a successful title always has imitators (in the 1970s, any mag with the word 'Woman's' in the name was guaranteed success: *Woman's Own*, *Woman's Realm*, *Woman's Teeth*, *Woman's Rifle*...)

That said, obviously, if your idea is original and you cannot make it less so, then you should continue. There are ways around cliché, too: Charles Palliser's extraordinary novels, set in the Victorian era, appear to merely pastiche Dickens and Wilkie Collins, but as the reader is led in, they offer up a darker and more awful world and ideas far removed from conventional Victoriana. Chris Morris' own *Four Lions* film uses the flipside of that device; as a comic movie, it's far more conventional than most of his work, because its central theme – the ordinariness of a group of suicide bombers – is in itself seen as problematic for a cinema audience.

(And an aside, on the topic of your brilliant idea, original or not; when you see the same idea on television, or in a film, or a book, or a hoarding, nine times out of ten you have not been ripped off. Someone else has had the same idea at the same time as you. It happens. Look at the history of the jet engine. Not now, obviously, this isn't a book about jet engines. Google it later.)

In short, any idea is a good idea. Don't be tied to the notion that you need a Brilliant Idea to write something; the idea can be the writing itself, or whichever format you've used (process is in itself an idea, from *Finnegan's Wake* to *The Blair Witch Project*, to something more modern I can't think of). And as I've said, you don't even need an idea to begin with, you can start writing and let an idea come.

But most of the time, if you want to write something, you will need an idea, and so we come to the next part of this chapter, which is where we came in: How Do You Get Ideas?

The easiest way to try and get an idea is often the worst; to sit down at a desk and tell yourself to have an idea. This is the easiest in the sense that you are focusing on your mission; and if the kind of idea you're after is the kind that can be sought out, that can be actually *found*, then it's a good one. Someone writing a book about tropical fish, for example, doesn't need to go on a creative writing course to get an idea for their latest book. They can just look around the room until they see their fish tank, observe that it contains guppies, and there it is, a new book, *The Life History of the Guppy*.

Or you can be very literal. You can triangulate the things you want – maybe they're the areas you're good on. The world is full of historical novels written by people who are fascinated by history and know how to make it come alive. My novel *Sparks* was a combination of interest in the internet, belief in randomness, and fondness for Douglas Adams novels. Some people deliberately pick an area they don't know about so they can combine learning with a fresh enthusiasm for their subject.

But what if you know that you can write, but nothing's coming? And – almost as bad – what if you've got an idea, and you've started to write, but you have no idea how to progress? (The great dilemma of being a fiction writer is that stories are places where the unexpected happens all the time, or even the impossible, and you're the one who has to think of all that.)

Well, if I can quote the great funk artist George Clinton: free your mind and your ass will follow. He was talking about dancing, I think, but the point pertains. Many writers have worked out techniques for freeing their minds and, as the great corpus of literature and the other great corpi of cinema, theatre, journalism and so on have demonstrated over the years, their asses have followed.

The trick is, of course, to get your mind off its normal course. (By this, I do not necessarily mean take drugs. Despite what you may have seen in films of the 1960s, drugs are not always creative and very often are anti-creative. After taking LSD for the first time, Paul McCartney got his roadie Mal Evans to write down an important statement. It was 'There are seven levels.') Forcing yourself to Have An Idea is a bit like looking at a Magic Eye drawing and hoping you will see some image or other.

Creative writers go to many lengths to have ideas. They walk across the pampas or the veldt. They submerge themselves in isolation tanks or refuse to speak to anyone for days. They disguise themselves as tinkers and wander the Orient for years. Well, all right, they don't necessarily but they do everything to escape the bounds of their normal lives. Not of course that you have to do that. Sometimes just going to the shops will do it. I had an offensive monologue about *Star Wars* come into to my mind fully formed one evening when I was walking the dog, and realised within seconds that this monologue, amazingly, would fit perfectly into a scene on a TV script I was working on. It's all a matter of letting go.

Situations where the mind roams free are incredibly productive. If you do exercise, that's a good situation (I would while away the tedium of a long swim by thinking about plots, but also by letting my mind nose around in itself like a weird self-consuming dog). If you're driving, or perhaps listening to music, or just with someone who's a bit dull, the mind will go off on its own and find things out.

All of which is fairly obvious, but the trick here is to not so much train the mind as encourage the mind to go off and retrieve ideas for you. It's as if, while you're not thinking of anything in particular, just letting thoughts scumble around in your brain, you have nevertheless put a mental marker in your head to pull out any interesting ideas that could be used for something later on. I won't give examples; suffice to say that it's not too hard to make random thoughts into little magnets which attract more useful thoughts (which is why it's never a waste of time to have a nap. Then one's mind is extremely loose and thoughts will drift in so rapidly you have to grab them before they evaporate).

Always have something on you to make a note of these ideas (maybe not if you're swimming). I make notes in my phone, but I also take a notebook and a pen with me whenever I'm out. I send myself baffling, misspelled emails to be deciphered later. Sometimes, if the idea is compact – like a sketch, or a poem, or a synopsis – I'll write the whole thing up at once, but mostly I'll just write 'Egg as president' or 'Watch taken from baby who turns out to benxbxmem'. Practise your handwriting (or turn on predictive texting).

Notes are always useful. Don't ever think that, because you had an idea six years ago and you're bored with your work from six years ago, that your old idea is no good, or that it's dated. Most ideas really don't date. Look at movies; they always appear shiny and contemporary, but the scripts they're made from have often been around for years. And you may even be ahead of your time, so your old idea has now become entirely contemporary simply by virtue of being around for a while.

Carry a pen or a computer, give yourself periods of time when you can free your mind, look at your own experiences (or imagine what it would be like to be someone else) and – here's a thing – remember that everything is grist to the mill. Just as the freelance reviewer is famously able to claim almost everything off tax (yes, even that *Friends* DVD) so the writer should be able to consume everything, from science to popular culture, from shipping law to what their mum thinks of next door's dog and – if not exactly recycle it in fictional form – use it somewhere. Because when you're writing, nothing is rubbish, nothing is irrelevant and nothing is useless (at this stage, obviously: you will have to edit at some point).

I think that the short reply to the great question-and-answer session question, 'Where do you get your ideas?' is, bluntly, 'No idea.' You can train your mind to recognize ideas, and you can put yourself in situations where ideas will be lured in, but I can't tell you why some people have creatively useful ideas and others don't.

In the end, it isn't 'where do you get your ideas?', it's 'how do you get your ideas?' And the answer to that question is probably: 'Practise.'

### Chapter Three
# Books and Publishing

I've written nine published books including an e-novel (*Sparks*), several comedy books (*Grumpy Old Men*, *The Dangerous Book for Middle-Aged Men*), some rock books and I co-wrote Eddie Izzard's autobiography with Eddie Izzard. The processes involved in all these books were always different. With the e-novel, things were understandably quite straightforward, as there were no middlemen or human filters involved. There are brilliant websites devoted to the whole process of getting your book online and you should consult those for details, but my brief guide would be this: make sure your book is sub-edited and proofed as well as you can do it (I am lucky enough to know a brilliant production editor and writer, Andy Fyfe) and make sure it has a decent cover design, to ensure it stands out from all the other little rectangles out there. *Sparks* has a brilliant yellow cover designed by Steven Appleby, who also did this book as well as a whole fleet of absurdly great cartoon and graphic masterpieces. Register with as many sites as possible, from iTunes to Smashwords (while reading the small print to see how much you'll get per copy and also who owns what). And publicise, publicise, and publicise again.

Self-publishing has many advantages but publicity is not one of them. An old-style publishing house brings with it PR (in varying degrees) and access to familiar outlets, like bookshops. A publisher will also pay you a different and generally smaller royalty, but might also give you an advance, so you can stay alive while you write your next book. They will also be more likely to reject your work, whereas the internet is defenceless against your talent.

That said, there is of course something lovely about holding your own book in your own hand. (Then again, there is something less lovely about hauling a box of your own unwanted books into the attic.) There are swings, therefore, and there are roundabouts.

The comedy books I've discussed before; suffice to say that you should always be aware of the sway that an unoriginal idea has with a publisher whilst simultaneously acknowledging the lure of an original idea for you as a writer. And the rock books and the Eddie Izzard book are examples of the golden rule that nothing you do as a writer will ever be irrelevant or useless. I was asked to do those books as a result of writing for the *NME*. My experience as a music journalist obviously helped there. I mean, durr. But also when it came to assisting Eddie Izzard with his autobiography, my experiences as an interviewer and as a comedy writer (the two don't always join up) worked in tandem. Which was nice.

I have however had less luck writing fiction for traditional print. I am the author of three and a half unpublished novels, probably because none of them were quite good enough for publication (especially the half one). But I keep writing them, and hope to start another quite soon.

With all this in mind, for the full publishing experience, I decided to speak to two of the best novelists I know, the writers Andrew Cartmel and Ben Aaronovitch.

Andrew Cartmel is a novelist, playwright, screenwriter, TV writer and script editor. He's also known for his work script-editing *Doctor Who*, and his novels, which range from the *Rupert Hood* spy thrillers to the brilliant *Vinyl Detective* series, are exciting, addictive and funny.

Ben Aaronovitch is also a novelist and television writer. He began his career writing *Doctor Who* (Andrew hired him) and has not only novelized his *Who* scripts but is perhaps best known for the brilliant supernatural police novels *Rivers of London*, *Moon Over Soho* and *Broken Homes*.

Andrew and Ben have known each other for a long time and would themselves be a great crime-fighting team. They're not just fantastic writers, they're absurdly entertaining company, which is one of the reasons I interviewed them together.

In the next few pages I guarantee you will find out everything you need to know about writing novels and getting them published or YOUR MONEY BACK.

I met Andrew and Ben in a sort of café place in North London, opposite a bookshop, appropriately, and barely had time to turn my recording device on before we were off...

**BA:** So what do you want to know about writing?

### DQ: How did you start?

**AC:** I got an agent who sold two of my scripts for a TV series... I created two television series, one was called *Down to Zero* and was about students who couldn't get a job after leaving college so they started a cult. And *Cheaters*, which was about kids who were going to fail their exams so they pulled off a heist at the examiner's office... And a year later my agent got me the job of script editor on *Doctor Who*.

**BA:** So there's me, and I thought what do I want to do with my life that doesn't involve a lot of work? I had no talents apart from writing. Someone gave me a good piece of advice; they said, look at the script editor at the end of the programmes you like and you send your work to that script editor. The idea being that if it has a name on it, it's much more likely to get through. I sent my script to the script editor on a show called *South of the Border* which was almost identical to the script I'd written. And then she said what do you like? I said, crime and science fiction, so she said write a script for (cop show) *Rockliffe's Babies* and a script for *Doctor Who* and I'll make sure they get them. And had *Rockliffe's Babies* not been cancelled... so at age twenty-four I was writing for *Doctor Who*.

**AC:** I read it, and within a few pages, I knew…

**BA:** There is an exact point where I decided to write the *Rivers…* books. I was working in Waterstones in Covent Garden and I was shelving science fiction novels that I'd never heard of, and I thought to myself, hold on, there are loads of these new authors, it must be a lot easier to write a novel than a TV script – I'll write a novel. And then I went home and – it's like Lego, you have a head full of ideas swirling around and you fit them together. Often one idea's not enough. It's usually two or three that fit together.

### I'm a book agent – what would put me off your submission?

**AC:** The trouble is, they want something that's the same as something that's been a big success, but also don't want something that's the same… Deep down inside, they're responding to the last trend.

**BA:** It's not enough for it to be good, someone has to fall in love with it. You always hear this phrase – 'I didn't fall in love with it…' They have to like it because they're going to spend a lot of time with it.

**AC:** It mustn't be too long. You don't want it to be much over 100,000 words.

**BA:** I think books are getting shorter. For Kindles. The need to take up six inches of the bookshelf is no longer there.

**AC:** In a few years, the relationship between books and Kindles will be like that between vinyl and mp3.

**BA:** Yeah. You'll be able to get the hardback with the Kindle but there won't be any paperbacks.

**Size is important?**

**BA:** What you've got to do is not scare them off. You must write in a good font, you must write double spaced…

**This seems to be a recurring theme in all aspects of writing, from movie scripts to books – appearance is really important.**

**BA:** Here's the thing – back when he was wading through the slush pile of *Doctor Who*, you could triage it really easily just by disposing of the ones that were written in crayon, they just never got read. Nowadays with the advent of Final Draft and Word for Windows…

**AC:** There's no excuse!

**BA:** There is just no excuse for not formatting your script or your novel in the correct way. The other thing is when you're submitting it to other people, read how they want it submitted and follow that to the letter. Because they're actually looking for an excuse not to accept it.

**AC:** And do not stick a big aggressive copyright notice on it. No professional writer in the world has ever done that. It's the hallmark of the amateur, and it suggests that you think they're going to steal your work. There used to be a notice in the script editing room –

# THE QUALITY OF THE WRITING IS ALWAYS IN INVERSE PROPORTION TO THE AMOUNT OF COPYRIGHT NOTICES ON THE SCRIPT.

**And you'll be lucky to get someone to read your idea, let alone steal it.**

**BA:** Jim Swallow said they're gonna steal your ideas, just live with it. If you have one good idea in your career, then you shouldn't really be doing writing.

**AC:** You have to be able to come up with another brilliant idea. If somebody steals your idea, it's because it's a good idea. I used to think you had a limited number of good ideas and if you had an idea stolen that would deplete your store of precious ideas. But Buñuel said, and this is a turning point in our lives as writers, the imagination is a muscle.

**This idea of guarding your little golden baby...**

**AC:** Forget it. Have lots of them!

**BA:** Especially when you're starting out.

**What's the best way to generate ideas?**

**BA:** I usually turn my computer off. I generally have my best ideas two seconds after I turn the computer off. I'm usually running out the door... I then phone him up and say, quick! You've got to remember this for me! He then writes it down on his computer and emails it back to me.

**AC:** Mindless activity. Washing the dishes is good, but it doesn't last long enough. Hoovering is very good. It takes about half an hour to hoover my house and I used to spend my hoovering time seething with rage over some slight my family had wrought on me and I suddenly realised I could spend the same time plotting. Also swimming.

**How much of an idea do you need before it really is an idea? I send myself incoherent notes like MAN IS WOMAN.**

**AC:** I've got three precepts and this leads us to one of them. When I get an idea now, I try and put down as much as I can quickly. I usually have some idea about the characters… instead of writing MAN IS WOMAN, I'd write something like 'Jesus Christ! She turned out to be a he – and I didn't mind!' I write it as dialogue, because then you're illuminating the character. When I started writing the idea was that when you came up with a character, you wrote a biography of the character: 'He likes opera, he grew up in Basingstoke…' By the time I finished the character was deader than a Victorian fucking stuffed animal. But if I can write one line of dialogue that comes from that character's mouth that reveals something, then I've got them. And they're alive.

The second precept of character is if you get a good name for the character you're halfway there.

**BA:** Oh yeah. And a good title. For a long time *Rivers of London* was *Magic Cops*, and that was a working title.

We really had to struggle to come up with a title. He came up with *Rivers of London*, and at the time it was, oh God, it's terrible but I can't think of anything better. And actually now, I love that title. But the second book, *Moon Over Soho*, I knew exactly the title. The sound of it…

**AC:** I find a really good title either comes right away or probably never. A great title is a joy forever. Ian Fleming, Raymond Chandler… magic at titles. *The Big Sleep*… The thing about the Bond titles is they're so familiar, we can't see them anymore. *From Russia, with Love* is an incredibly good title.

**BA:** And this also applies to chapter titles. If you're the kind of person who likes chapter titles, and I am, if you can come up with a chapter title, you've pretty much written the chapter in your head.

**What's a good chapter title for you?**

**BA:** I had someone murdered in the Groucho Club, so the chapter title was *One Tenth of My Ashes*, one of Groucho Marx's quotes – 'when I die, my agent will get one tenth of my ashes.'

**AC:** This leads to my final writing precept. I like to visualize the whole thing when I'm writing, so I take a piece of A4 paper and I turn it on its side and draw a grid across it. You end up with nine boxes, or sixteen boxes, and you try and work out what box of story falls where. It helps to pace the story, roughly. I don't do that anymore because thanks to the chapter titles what I now do is have a folder for the book and if there's going to be fifteen chapters for the book, I create fifteen word files and give them each a chapter name and I can move them around and I can see the whole book at a glance.

**BA:** There are programs that do that. Scrivener's very good.

**What about treatments?**

**AC:** A treatment is a bit like a short story, except it's written in the present tense.

**BA:** A treatment is also a problem because it's now the point at which the gibbons interfere with your script the most because they're too lazy to read the whole script. But it's also very useful. I've got a very good friend who writes very long treatments for his books, and I don't, because none of my treatments have ever survived five minutes' contact with my brain. So nearly always for me the content is what happens at the beginning, what happens in the middle and what happens at the end, in a very big way. When I was writing *Broken Homes*, I knew it started with an accident at the beginning, I knew halfway through it they would find out about X and I knew at the end Y would happen… If you've got those three anchors, you can write a book. I don't really start writing a book until I have those three anchors.

**AC:** But you have to bear in mind everybody's different.

**There's the Larkin line about writing a novel being a journey where you know the beginning and the end and some of the places on the way...**

**AC:** I once had a revelation which was exactly that. Driving across a desert and there's various points you can see... Landmarks on the way.

**BA:** But this leads us to the most important thing, which is this. It is almost impossible to write for a market. I don't care what all these books say. I've never heard anyone successfully write for a market.

**AC:** You mustn't try and second guess what will sell. You have to write what turns you on, no matter how weird that is.

**BA:** And if it doesn't sell, that's because you're too weird. But you cannot write a novel fast enough to catch the zeitgeist, to catch a trend. Because the time to be writing a *50 Shades of Grey* rip-off was about three months before the book came out. So you write what you like and you hope that somebody else likes it. It's that simple. And it's that depressing in a way. Because it is possible to be quite a good writer, writing stuff you like, and no one will like it.

If I have one word of wisdom it's this... You can do it with a script. Scripts are different from books. For a start it only takes a week and a half to write a good script, if you know what you're doing. Two, a script is not a work of art. It is a recipe for something else. It's a collaborative process and you don't have to dot every i and cross every t. You do not necessarily want your script to be perfect, because for a start you need a few niggles for the producer to take out. Whereas a book, that is your work, once it's done and you write 'The End' and send it off, that is it. So it is your voice.

## How much is a book a collaborative effort?

**BA:** As little as you can get away with.

**AC:** You really don't want the agent's notes, you really don't want the editor's notes. You need somebody to tell you – for instance, I've just written a book and someone said, 'You've written, "He didn't give him a second glass," did you mean, "He didn't give him a second glance"?'

**BA:** What you don't want is – 'We need it to be 20% funnier.'

**AC:** 'It doesn't jump off the page.'

**BA:** 'It's not exciting enough.' These are all fucking useless. But you cannot always choose.

**AC:** What you really need is a cluster of friends. When you're starting out as a writer you really want three or four people – you need more than one or two because if one person says something to you, you may think, 'I'm not going to change that,' but if two people say it to you, you must make that change.

I listen to two kinds of notes. Where people say something and it rings a bell, where I half thought of that myself, or when I'll make a change that I'm highly resistant to.

**BA:** I get this from translators quite a lot, they say, 'Peter Grant says this, what does it mean?' and I say, 'I can't remember!' And it made sense at the time and I don't want to take it out of the book, but I just can't remember. You can't do that to translators because a translator needs to know what the intent was behind the words.

### Advice for young novelists?

**AC:** Always go with your gut. Never send it out to the world until you've shown it to three or four friends who are likely to be ruthless. Not ardent admirers who are going to love it. Not your mum, unless your mum actually can be objective. Because the first thing you do is unlikely to be good enough to be sent out. You're going to find some agents and target them – you don't want to waste your shot with a bad book. So get several people to read it and if they say this isn't good enough, don't send it out, do another one. John Fowles wrote four books before he thought he was good enough to send any out.

**BA:** And put it down and read it again three months later. Or an arbitrary length of time, but it's got to be longer than two weeks.

**AC:** The instant you finish a book, start another one. Because the first one's liable to die under fire and you want to fall in love with the next one. Then go back to the first one.

**BA:** Conversely, always make sure you have two paragraphs of the second and third books ready to go when you send the first one out. If it's a series, always have the next two paragraphs.

**AC:** But if you've done your job well at all, your characters will be sufficiently alive in your mind, you're already thinking about the next one.

**BA:** Don't worry about subtext. Take care of text and the subtext will take care of itself. Because the subtext actually comes out of your own obsessions, so whatever you're obsessed with will come out in the subtext anyway. Notebook! Have we mentioned how important it is to carry a notebook? Carry a notebook!

**AC:** And write down bits of dialogue.

**BA:** Cos that thing you think you'll never forget, you'll forget.

**AC:** And it's also great for writing down names.

**BA:** Names. Names! Names! Names are a real pain. I don't know about other people but I completely stall until I've got the name of a character. So every time you see a good name like in the credits of a film or in a book or in his case, *New Scientist*... Because they're real people.

**AC:** At the very most basic, if you've got someone with an unusual name – and I'm not talking about strainingly bizarre Dickensian names – even if your reader has forgotten who the character is, they'll remember the name. 'Doctor Meatcane – I can't remember who he is but I'll remember in a minute.' It's really useful. And Meatcane by the way was a real name.

**BA:** Oh, one of the things to do when you edit your manuscript three months later is take out all the times you've over-used that really clever phrase.

**AC:** My new book's about a killer who's really painstaking about covering his tracks, and I had to take out all the times I'd used 'carefully' and 'painstakingly'.

**BA:** Don't do modernism for your first book. Don't do a book where you don't use the letter A.

## Three best and three worst things about being a writer...

**AC:** The three worst things are no pay, no money and no pay. People used to talk about writer's block and I've never had it but what I've always had is writer's pay block. The best thing about being a writer is working at home.

**BA:** The best thing about being a writer is being paid to do something you love to do, and in fact something you're pretty much forced to do by your psyche.

**AC:** I read this Thomas Berger book in which he was talking about someone who discovered after a while they became vaguely ill if they didn't write every day. And some of the worst things about being a writer are also some of the best things. You know, one of the worst things is you can never switch it off and everything becomes material…

**BA:** And one of the best things is – you can never switch it off and everything becomes material!

**And finally… there's a Borges story about a writer about to be shot and he wishes for God to stop time so he can compose his last play in his head. Apart from being shot, would that be satisfactory to you?**

**BA:** No, because the main validation a writer craves is the paypacket.

**AC:** Ha ha! Well put!

### Chapter Four

# Comedy and Performance

A nd no, there won't be a chapter called *Tragedy and Performance*. Because you know the line: comedy is tragedy plus time. Also tragedy is when I hit your thumb with a hammer, or when you burst into flames for no apparent reason and run around screaming, 'Help! I'm on fire and I don't know why!' And of course writing narrative comedy is no different to writing narrative drama, except you have to be funny as well. And so on. So tragedy and drama, easy. Comedy, much harder.

Of course, with comedy, it helps to be funny. There's nothing more annoying to a writer than working for weeks on the perfect one-liner and then seeing a man in a pub make everyone collapse laughing just by making a face (the only thing more annoying is working for weeks on the perfect one-liner and seeing an actor change the words so it's not funny. No wait, the only thing more annoying is having a producer not understand the joke in the first place because it's a joke and they don't really get jokes). Being funny isn't always down to writing funny things (the great American humorist and why-am-I-explaining-who-he-is James Thurber once co-wrote a play full of epigrams and wit which went down like a lead balloon. The only line that got a laugh, he noted later, was 'Thank you.') but it does help.

The writer differs in this from the performer. You don't have to be funny in person to be a funny writer. Maybe you're too shy or you forget the joke or you would just rather someone else got a custard pie in their face. Perhaps your humour doesn't work on panel games where stand-ups shout aggressively at each other about their genitals. Possibly you suffer massively from *mal de l'esprit de l'escalier* and can only think of a joke half an hour after everyone else (this is no bad thing; being the person who says the first funny thing that comes into your head also makes you the most annoying, I find). Some comedy writers, like me, are loud and annoying. Others are quiet, and this is often better.

Comedy writing takes many forms. For performers, it has one central theme: them. Performers write comedy in many different ways – as stand-up which they perform, as sitcom in which they star, as sketches in which they appear, and so on, but it's rare that a performer will write a piece which doesn't include them (Alan Bennett and Victoria Wood being classically great examples of this, while more recent examples of self-hiring being done remarkably well include *Miranda*, the various members of The League of Gentlemen and *Mrs Brown's Boys*.

There are two very good reasons to write and perform your own material. One is common sense; you can hear it in your head, you know how it's meant to sound and it's probably about you anyway. The brilliant Reeves and Mortimer have at various times assembled troupes of sympathetic actors and comics, but nobody does Vic and Bob's material better than they do. The other reason is less obvious; if you want to promote your own career, promoting yourself advances every aspect of that career. People – and by 'people' I mean producers and commissioning editors – tend to notice performers more than writers. It's obvious why. Performers are there, on your TV and radio and stage. They have familiar faces and voices. They are memorable. Writers are names on pieces of paper. If they have a recognizably different style, a producer will only know this by watching a show or reading a script all the way through. And this never happens. (A producer friend of mine only managed to get a BBC head of department to listen to a fifteen minute radio show I'd made by actually putting the CD on in his office. And even then, that only means he heard it as one might hear far-off birdsong.)

If you can, if you have some self-confidence and even a gram of acting or performing ability, appear in your own work. It's a lot easier that way.

If you don't want to appear in your own work, fair enough. (There will be a chapter about writing and not performing later on.) But be prepared to spend your entire career being Judged By The Last Thing You Did. You may be aware of the old saw that you're only as big as the last thing you did; partly this is true because people only care about your current status, not the great show you made in 2001. But it's also true because nobody remembers anything that happened more than a week ago.

Over the years I've written many potted bios and CVs; and it's weird to watch them go from 'David Quantick has written for that show everyone liked in the Eighties' to 'David Quantick is writing for that funny man who does jokes about Britpop' to 'David Quantick is now writing for a really modern thing.' You feel like the mannequin in the film of H.G. Wells' *Time Machine*: as the years race by, the fashions change but the mannequin remains the same. When people say that you have to constantly update your CV, they really mean that you constantly have to update yourself.

For now, though, let's assume you're a writer and performer (we'll come on to the kids who forgot their gym kit later). We're assuming you have either the talent or the ego or both to stand on a stage or in front of a camera and deliver lines you've written for yourself to deliver. And we'll take the most primitive form of writing first: stand-up.

I have some experience of stand-up. As well as writing for several stand-up comedians over the years and 'co-writing' (ie transcribing his brilliance) Eddie

Izzard's autobiography, I once performed a series of gigs as a stand-up for a men's magazine (and also, out of curiosity, to see if I could be a stand-up comedian). It was an interesting experience; the first show I played was a talent contest and I won. The second show I played I don't recall. The third show I played was the notoriously ebullient venue Camden Jongleurs. Just before I came onstage the compère tore up a birthday card by way of explaining he didn't do birthday greetings and then I went on. Ten seconds later, halfway through my first joke, someone heckled me, forcibly. One second later, the entire room was shouting at me suggesting powerfully that I leave the stage. I did so, and my abiding memory of the evening as I left was a woman taking time off from eating her dinner to shout at me that I was terrible (not her exact words).

I did a couple more, less stressful shows but decided that stand-up was not for me. Apart from the sheer being-shouted-at-ness of it all, I felt I would, if lucky, be one of those comics whose material is good but whose performance is never more than adequate. I also didn't want to put in the hours, weeks and months of gigging, touring, writing and practise it would take to become adequate. And I found the atmosphere bleak.

Backstage at a rock concert, when more than one band is playing, generally there's a pleasant ambience. Musicians are rivalrous (it's a word) but they tend to mix well, enjoying the company of people who do the same job (writers are the same). But backstage at a stand-up show is different. There's a lot of sniping between performers, a lot of edginess and a general awareness that if someone does well that night, everyone else will be the loser. Stand-ups, as intelligent, ambitious, and insecure people usually are, tend to be envious, jealous people wedded to the old Gore Vidal maxim ('It is not enough to succeed: others must fail'). And this despite the fact that most of them are lovely people outside the venues. Really. They just don't always play well backstage.

So the basics of stand-up, from the point of view of someone who's only done it five times:

**Have material**. Even if you're the new Frankie Howerd, and can do an hour riffing on one sentence, have that sentence. And probably some other ones too.

**Work out who you're going to be.** Are you a collection of one-liners? Are you a reminiscing bundle of nostalgic anecdotes? Are you a spewing hate machine? Are you a surreal stream of consciousness? You will possibly take some time to find out what your act is – and even if it's you being you, it's still an act. That's why it's called an act. It's an act. But it's never too early to start.

**Do a lot of gigs.** If you're going to play stadiums, you're going to play pubs first. Every show you do (a gig is a show, from jazz) is

Nietszchean, in that if it does not destroy you, it will make you stronger. And be selective in what you take from an audience. If they love your impression of a famous TV comic, unfortunately that doesn't matter because if you get on TV, you won't be doing that. If they like your routine about accountants, that may be because you too are an accountant and you're playing your work do. Similarly, if they hate your jokes about structuralism and Roland Barthes, then that's possibly because you're playing Camden Jongleurs on a Friday night (or because your audience are semioticians and don't like where you're coming from).

**Refine all the time.** Make a note of what works and what doesn't. Decide what you should keep in and what you should lose. Edit, shorten, fill the gaps with new material, and repeat until funnier.

**Remember you're the one who has to say all this, so make it actually sayable.** Eddie Izzard is dyslexic, meaning in his case he had to learn his routines by rote, repeating them to himself. This meant his verbal dexterity was tempered by the fact that, to paraphrase Harrison Ford in the popular children's film *Star Wars*, he had to say the words. A lot of writers starting out, high on language and funny formations, tend to write elaborate, wordy dialogue with lots of subclauses, nouns, adjectives and wah in it. A good rule for a spoken sentence is it shouldn't really have more than two verbs in it, or sound like it needs brackets. Yes, funny sentences are funny but if you can't say it (or if you've been booed offstage before you've completed your sentence) you should be back home rewriting the works of Henry James. There's a good reason that one-liners are popular (and why even Oscar Wilde was fond of a snappy epigram). As the pop group Roxette memorably put it, 'Don't bore us / Get to the chorus.'

**Have a strand.** Callbacks are always fun – jokes which refer to a remark you made earlier. Stories can build, return to themes already mentioned, and if you can include your audience in the narrative (i.e. tell a story they like) you'll take them with you all the way to a huge notional bank.

The rest is up to you. To be honest, I'd ask around; find someone who didn't get booed offstage within ten seconds. And it is all down to you in the end. A somewhat different area is sketch comedy, which I will be looking at later; this has the great advantage that normally the audience watching you have come along or tuned in specifically to see your act and not someone else. I will be looking at this in the chapter about writing comedy (as opposed to writing and performing it), but I mention it as a bridge into writing and performing comedy on the radio and TV.

This differs from stand-up in many ways. For a start, you may well be part of a team of people. You might be a character comic (which is still a major part of stand-up, too: look at Harry Hill and Al Murray's Pub Landlord, both brilliant comic creations who work just as well in a club as on TV). You might be performing live sketches, which is how the League of Gentlemen began. You might be a ventriloquist (surprisingly popular in a way). In any of those cases, you'll be generating material in a different way from a stand-up comedian.

That is to say, you'll be writing it, possibly in a team, but always for a character, who may or may not be an exaggerated version of you. Again I will be looking at sketch and performance comedy later, but for now I would say please God make it funny as well as 'well-observed'. Comics who play characters often get all the details right but forget to add a comic angle as well: they sometimes (perhaps literally) fall in love with the characters, which as they're playing the characters, rather dubiously means they've fallen in love with themselves. So if you do have a Wonderful Old Woman character or a Loveable Nerd, in the name of heaven remind yourself that other people have to find this delightful impersonation entertaining as well.

Which reminds me of the devil's work in its most distilled form: improv. I am slightly joking, but improv – which is short for improvisation and long for everyone watching it – is one of the most overrated forms of 'writing' known to humanity. It makes mime and juggling look like rigorous haiku composition. The idea, if you've been out, is this: actors and comics don't write anything down, they just start to act out scenes, creating characters and dialogue as they go. The fact that writers can take months to plan a story and people it with convincing characters is neither here nor there with the improv fan. Spontaneity is more important than cohesiveness.

'We know why you hate improv,' says my wife, 'Because it puts you out of a job.' She's right, of course. And I hate improv because I have wasted days, actual days, transcribing the waffle of actors who think that pretending to be cats or riding imaginary hobby horses for two hours is the best way to invent four seconds of funny dialogue. It's not. It's the comic equivalent of trying to write the plays of Oscar Wilde using only consonants. It's a waste of time. Anything funny you have to say, you can think of sitting down at a desk with a pen and paper. If it takes you four hours, three actors and a fit of giggling, you're probably not funny. And just as you wouldn't buy a book which had been made up as it went along, contained loads of dead ends that hadn't been edited out and didn't have a proper plot because you can't really make up a complex story as you go along, so you wouldn't waste your time with an improvised comedy or acted piece (if you would, then you are clearly an actor and I claim my days, actual days, back).

That said, I have seen improv work brilliantly. Used around an existing script, improv allows actors to contribute new ideas, flesh out characters and get a feel for the piece which a writer (static, behind a desk) doesn't always appreciate. As part of the writing process it can be extremely valuable. Just not as a replacement for the writing process. And of course the work of Christopher Guest (*Spinal Tap*) and Mike Leigh (*Topsy-Turvy*) shows that improvisation, if layered, checked, rehearsed and honed, can be very effective (although neither of these two admittedly brilliant talents are too hot on plot and story. Ooh, controversial). And you may of course find improvisation useful to develop a character or loosen yourself up mentally. That's great, just transcribe it yourself, OK? You want to be a writer, do some writing.

And now performing not in character. By which I mean a lot of things. I have presented several radio shows, often as myself but sometimes in variations of myself, depending who it's for. On my Radio 2 show *The Blagger's Guide*, I am loud, aggressive and annoying, because I want the show to be loud, aggressive and annoying. On the rare occasions I present a straight documentary (cf. *Reality Is An Illusion Caused By Lack of N.F. Simpson*, which I mention largely to namecheck the brilliant surreal philosopher and playwright Wally Simpson), I write as and sound like a more reasoned, rational person, because I don't want my personality to get in the way of the content. And when by some weird accident of nature I was the voice of Channel Four's popular daytime show *Coach Trip*, I raved like a hung-over David Frost in a gale (one day I'll tell you about how I found out I'd been replaced on that show in an email sent to a third party and what the producer really thought of me. But I digress, you bet). I've also hosted a massively unpopular radio show called *Broken Arts*, where I played a presenter version of myself (how unpopular? I tuned into a Radio Four complaints show one day and heard the announcer say, 'And if you're David Quantick, you might want to cover your ears.' He was right, too).

The point is, there is a massive middle ground between Playing A Character and Being Yourself. Everyone, from chat show hosts to current affairs reporters, occupies that middle ground. Just watch a local news reporter coming to the end of an outside broadcast filmed in bad weather and observe the relish with which they say, 'This is Jane Smith, reporting for Local News, in the teeth of a gale, tonight.' Because they're getting to play the part of a news reporter in the teeth of a gale. Look at the weather man or woman, working on the balance between being Perky And Fun and About To Report A Major Weather Catastrophe. As someone said, it's all showbiz.

So if you're lucky enough or bright enough to write the words that you say, don't mess around worrying about starting with 'This is…' or 'Welcome to…' or that sort of pootling detail. Work out who you are being. Are you Warm And Witty? Droll But Loveable? Very Angry? Intellectual? Once you have decided which version of yourself you want to put across, the rest is easy. You're like an actor improvising a part, except you've written it down and you don't keep getting the giggles. Look at TV chat shows – some hosts like to be the star, joining in little skits and set-ups with their guests. Other hosts like to be the professional interviewer, getting the truth out of their guests. The American model is more of a comedy show where famous people drop in from time to time. Watch *Newsnight* to see how the presenters play with the concept of being serious – are they going to be rather bland, letting the facts speak for themselves, or are they going to be inquisitors, the Cardinal Richelieu of the swivel chair? Everyone on television and radio is a performer, presenting a controlled version of themselves, and if that's where you'd like to be, the sooner you work out who you 'are', the better.

And finally, speeches. I've been a best man and I've written speeches for people who didn't feel they could write their own. It was fun working out how to do that, so I'm briefly going to share the secrets of wedding speeches (or any speeches). Firstly, work out what needs to be said. This sounds obvious (it is obvious, is why) but it's amazing how many speeches end with the speaker suddenly blurting, 'Oh I forgot, thanks to the bridesmaids' or 'I should have said before, this isn't a drill, the building really is on fire.' Marshal your points. If you're writing a speech for a best man or similar, ask the speaker for some stories and facts. I wrote one for a friend who was giving away his daughter in marriage. I asked him for the story of how she and her husband met, some facts about her life, some stories, moments he was proud of, things he found annoying about the groom, and how he was feeling right now. Then you stick all those things together in a pleasing order, add a conclusion, and thank the bridesmaids.

Same goes for any spoken piece which is largely made of references. Do a bit of research and you'll look, sound and be convincing. The most horrific example of how effective this approach can be is the corporate gig. This is a particularly undelightful but apparently well-paid event where stand-up comedians are hired to entertain drunk people who've never heard of them. Most comics of my acquaintance have done them and they all say the same thing; abandon all subtlety and wit, and just get a list of the people in the company who can be mocked. Then do jokes about them by name based on their alleged greediness, stupidity, poor taste in clothing, and so on.

That last section is one of the many reasons that a lot of writers find that they are happier behind a keyboard, writing for other people's voices. Or perhaps their style is so adaptable they don't feel they have just the one voice. Maybe you feel that your confidence doesn't extend to speaking in public (this is a shame; the world is full of confident people who have no writing talent, so why not acknowledge that if you can write the words, you can say them, and go out and say them?) Either way, the next chapter is for you.

(And yes, there are two chapters about comedy writing. I'm a comedy writer.)

## Chapter Five
# Writing Comedy

There is no job more glamorous than comedy-writing. As I type these words, I am sitting in a small windowless room that smells of long-dead sandwiches as another writer works on a laptop. We have been hired on a day rate to come up with funny things for a celebrity to say to other celebrities. It's not a bad job at all, even though I would rather be doing it at home, and I have been asked to come in for eight hours to do what would take a puppy dog about two hours to do. So you see that a) comedy-writing is not all that glamorous and b) I can moan about anything.

Writing comedy, though, is mostly this: sitting in small windowless, slightly smelly rooms, coming up with lines. Which is, incidentally the hardest sort of thing to write. The difficult bit for a writer is coming up with an idea. Once you have a good idea, you can write and write and write. This is why sitcoms are so brilliant for writers; if you've got the kernel of an idea for a regular, returning, repetitive comedy – that one idea – you can keep it going for years until it runs out of steam. Shows as diverse as *Curb Your Enthusiasm*, *Dad's Army*, *Frasier* and *The IT Crowd* had such strong central conceits that they deserved longevity just to explore all the aspects of that central conceit. (That said, my dream is to see an episode of *My Mother The Car*, an American sitcom about a man whose mother was reincarnated as an automobile, and he drove around in her a lot. Actually, my dream is to see episode nine, because how did they get that far?)

One idea is hard to have but if it'll keep a series going for years it's worth it. The same with a film idea, or a book or a play. A strong idea which draws people in and makes them say, 'Ooh, I want some of that' not only makes your work good, but it reduces your workload. Because it's not the amount of writing you have to do that kills you, it's the amount of ideas. The hardest job for a writer is coming up not with an idea singular, but ideas plural. And writing lines is horrible, because it means that every sentence you write – every single one – has to contain a new idea.

It's the same with sketch shows. One of the great things about creating a recurring character is, again, that you only need one idea and you can then explore it at will. A sketch show without recurring characters is hell to write, because – yes – every sketch has to contain a new idea. And having ideas hurts the brain. And it's the same – I might as well mention them here – with writing scripts for awards shows. Not, you might think, the most common job, but it exists and someone does it. I've done it. It's weird. Not only do you have to come up with a different idea for each bit of presentation but you also have to conform to whatever the awards show's guidelines are. My least favourite experience here would be working on a presenter's script for the BAFTAs a few years ago. As a comedy writer, you tend to use mockery and the odd dig when writing; however, when writing the BAFTA script, I was told that you can't be rude about anyone. Try writing anything funny about someone without being at all rude. It can be done, but it's very difficult; which is why the BAFTA scripts tend to contain lines like 'And now a man whose talent is even more amazing than his looks…' and so forth.

So writing lines (an apt phrase) is the hardest job. It can be fantastic, however, in the right circumstances. I've read about the writers on the Bing Crosby and Bob Hope *Road* movies. Bob Hope would be given a great line to say by his writers, which would cause Bing Crosby to make his writers give him a better line, which in turn would make Hope… The competitive edge for the writers and the stars is what makes those films so crammed with brilliant lines. And working on shows like *The Thick of It* and *Veep*, which are written and rewritten by different (and really good) writers does make it a pleasure and a challenge to come up with good dialogue.

A moment, then, to talk about the American writers' room. 'Why don't we have it here?' a lot of people say in the UK, using a strange kind of logic that goes like this: America sitcoms are great and British sitcoms aren't, and American sitcoms have writers' rooms and British ones don't, so it follows that if British sitcoms had writers' rooms, they'd be great. There are every kinds of things wrong with this statement. For a start it assumes that all American sitcoms are great, when they're certainly not. Lots of them are awful and some of the ones that aren't awful are annoying. But what they do have is a rigorousness and a sense of process that non-American shows lack. That is to say, they conform a lot more to things. They conform to conventional writing guides a lot more, they follow the rules of story and character and they talk about Story Arc and Beats and so forth. This is mostly a good thing, as it keeps writers from being sloppy (a major issue with British sitcom) and it ensures that your show has a rhythm and a satisfying shape, much as a good song has verses and a chorus and a symphony has movements and a climax. But it can also be restrictive and formulaic and so when we say that 'even the worst American sitcom has structure and is coherent' we are also in some ways praising an animated corpse; it can walk and it can get out of bed and go to the shops but it's still dead.

The writers' room is the holy grail of sitcom fetishists. It's not so much a room as the idea that a room full of writers is better than a room with one writer in it, or two (the traditional British model). The logic here is not only that writers will try and cap each other's jokes, improving and evolving the comedy just as weapons technology improves and evolves during a war, but also that by working and reworking story and character, at speed, under pressure, a better show will be produced. By and large, this is true, but it only happens in America for one reason; they've got the money. Paying ten writers is, unsurprisingly, ten times more expensive than paying one writer. In the US, where advertising funds television, a show has more money to spend on people (sitcoms, fortunately, rarely require expensive sets) and so they do. American and British crews are roughly as good, American directors and British probably the same, American producers and British I wouldn't like to say, but American writers – over-worked and burnt out as they often become – get paid a lot of money. British writers don't.

Which is why, in this aside, I am advising you to think very carefully about writing as part of a duo if you're British. The comedy writing pair has two advantages; one, you have a mutual support network and two, if you've got the balance right, you'll make better scripts. By balance, I mean this: there is no point you teaming up if you're both only funny. You need two funny writers like a car needs two horns. The best writing duos – most notably *the best* writing duo, Dick

Clement and Ian La Frenais – are made up of one funny writer and one writer who can do story. This is a lot more useful. But do it your own way. It works for lots of great teams in the UK. Oh, and you split the money down the middle. That's always annoying.

Aside over, the writers' room has been tried in the UK (presumably on a lower budget). And it can work. *The Thick of It* used a rotating system of writers, polishing and rewriting as it went, creating what producer, creator and genius Armando Iannucci calls 'a lovely stew' of comedy. But it's not a roomful of writers throwing one-liners about and making it up as they go along. The traditionalist sitcom *My Family* claimed to use a writers' room but as nobody involved in that show has lived to tell the tale, we have no information about whether it worked or not (or maybe I just didn't ask anyone). It was however, as I say, very traditional.

Assuming you're a British writer, whether there's one of you or not, your comedy goals are to write either a sitcom or a film. You could create a sketch show but, as the brilliant *Big Train* showed, no matter how good your show is, if you only write it and don't perform in it, people won't really care. Performer-driven sketch shows are easier to market, easier to remember, and generally easier to like (although this applies less on radio, as I found with my series *One* on Radio 4). Or maybe if you've got an idea for a comedy drama, you should go with it, because while a weird and shifting quicksand,

the hinterland between comedy and other genres –
comedy thrillers, comedy spy shows, comedy romances
– is a popular one and the balance between the laffs and
the other stuff is always appealing. But be prepared to
subsume your talent for gags in the story (and indeed
vice versa).

Let's deal with sitcoms first, as those are the scripts
I'm sent the most by new writers. We'll come on to
film in general in a later chapter, in which I interview
someone who's had several movie scripts made (and
one turned into a hit Broadway musical). Sitcoms have
been the backbone of comedy for many years and as
an artform have been perfected and reinvented in
pretty much every decade. As a format, they include
everything from *Hancock* (a monologuist drifts into
mundane situations and makes them weirder) to
*Roseanne* (a malicious feminist tortures her family in
brilliantly funny ways) from *The Office* (everyone is
embarrassed in a fake fly-on-the-wall documentary) to
*Dad's Army* (the pettiness of small-town life makes even
the threat of mass extermination funny), from *The Big
Bang Theory* (clever people are stupid) to *Frasier* (clever
people are really stupid).

Sitcoms can contain anything. They can develop
narratives over years – the sheer longevity of the initially
cartoonish *Only Fools and Horses* forced it to become
a family saga and created a unique balance of goonish
poignancy – or they can be relentlessly unchanging, like

the superb *Father Ted*, a show whose weekly premise was almost always 'A quirky priest comes to stay.' They can claim to break boundaries while actually erecting them (*Love Thy Neighbour*) and they can appear to be supernatural nonsense which is really social commentary (*Being Human*. It's a flatshare sitcom). They can be glossy (*Friends*), scabby (*Bottom*), proudly bizarre (*House of Fools*), oddly conventional (*Outnumbered*) or just wonderful (*Frasier, Roseanne, Fawlty Towers, Father Ted, The Simpsons, I'm Alan Partridge, Dad's Army, Misfits, Porridge, Modern Family, The Big Bang Theory* and that one you like). They can be sentimental, angry, stupid, exciting, boring, static, animated, arty, laugh-tracked, audience-less, or anything, so long as they're funny.

You'd be mad if you'd never ever, as a writer, thought of writing one. They're also a great discipline as they do have certain boundaries. They're generally between twenty-two (America) and thirty (BBC) minutes long. They usually feature a limited amount of sets (room with sofa, bar or café, workplace, occasional others). They have a regular cast. And best of all, the thrilling thing which makes them different from films and soap operas and dramas and every other narrative form, they are entirely dedicated to the maintenance of stasis. In other words, where you are at the end of the episode is the same as where you were at the beginning. Of course there are exceptions to this – like I say, a long-running series will have a long-term development, while some shows enjoy an element of change – but the general rule is this: if you start your episode with three idiots working in a chip shop who have no love life and no money, you can do what you like in the middle – the idiots find a diamond ring, develop superpowers, became slaves to a sentient egg, whatever – but generally you will also end your episode with three idiots working in a chip shop who have no money or no love life. (One of the great sitcom finales of all time is the very last episode of *Seinfeld*, in which the main characters end up alone, isolated and picking up on the exact same conversation they were having at the start of the very first episode. A point, being made, brilliantly.)

Stasis is against the usual rules of drama. Drama is all about change – people growing as individuals, heroes achieving their destiny, villains realizing their doom, flawed figures hurtling towards tragedy. (Famously, one of the problems filming the *Judge Dredd* stories has always been that Hollywood movies require a character to change and grow; Dredd's brilliance is that he never changes. He is, like the Terminator, like the Juggernaut, like Norman Wisdom, relentless and this is why we like him.)

Stories normally resolve. Sherlock Holmes doesn't give up solving the case, the crew of the Enterprise never pop home for a lie-down, King Lear doesn't calm down, and so on. Each story goes on until it's all sorted out. Someone, I wish I could remember who, once said that all stories are explanations. This is brilliant; but it doesn't apply to sitcoms, possibly because in a sitcom there's no explanation necessary. You know who you're watching, you know how they would react to a given situation, and if you don't, it's not a sitcom.

Writing a sitcom, then, isn't like telling a story, it's telling a situation (hence the name). The story of *The Three Bears* doesn't start until they leave the house and Goldilocks finds the door open. But the sitcom of *The Three Bears* is entirely contained in the words 'Once upon a time, there were three bears.' After that, you can do anything. Goldilocks can come over and rob them. A priest bear can come to stay. One of the bears can be stuck at home all day. Anything.

Which reminds me. There are two great dim clichés of sitcom criticism which you need to dismiss. One is this: 'All great sitcoms have only twelve episodes.' This is drivel, and it actually means, 'I am so classy that the only sitcoms I like are *Fawlty Towers*, *Father Ted* and *The Office*.' Loads of great sitcoms have tens, even hundreds, of episodes.

The other cliché is, 'It's really hard to write an episode with just one character.' You know the one they mean, where our hero is locked in the toilet, or in a lighthouse, or confined to bed, or some other scenario where the rest of the cast are ill or they've gone over budget and the entire episode is the central character doing stuff alone. This is seen as a kind of master class of writing when in reality it's not that hard to write a story for one character for half an hour. She gets up, she's stuck, she thinks about things, she goes through a variety of emotions, she is rescued, she's back to square one. Not so hard. What's hard is writing a story for two to five characters, probably with a B and C plot, which is both fresh and logical, which lasts for half an hour without either running out of steam or finds itself cramming in too much plot. (A sitcom can have no incident, or some incident, but only peak *Frasier* could really do full-on bed-hopping, window-leaving-through French farce. Give it a go, though.)

Writing a sitcom, then. Start where you like, but you will need the following: characters, a situation, and stories. It sounds obvious, but people do go wrong at the first hurdle, and think that things like this will sustain a sitcom:

Just being funny.

Turning on the camera and seeing what happens.

Describing the life of me and my mates.

Stories about my old job, of which I have loads and they are hilarious.

Mocking the dead format that is sitcom.

Stories about my old job, of which I have loads and they are *hilarious*.

Gentle Jesus (to quote the 90s group Earl Brutus), make it stop. These are all terrible ideas. Admittedly none of them are that common, but I needed examples for a list and that was all I had. So to dismiss in turn:

**Just being funny.** This assumes that a sitcom is a monologue or a conversation. It isn't. Every sitcom needs a story, even if that story is plug basic. No matter how funny your video recording of one or more people being funny is, it isn't a sitcom (and if it's half an hour long, it's probably not funny either).

**Turning on the camera and seeing what happens.** Pretty much the same awful thing as just being funny, except there is some room for plot and character and maybe even story. But you're going to end up with the TV equivalent of a story told by a little child: 'Once there was a man, it was me, and he was late, and then a dragon, the end.' Planning and structure and all that, please.

**Describing the life of me and my mates.** Because we're really funny. The things we say! Unbelievable! I bet. I bet they're very much like the things everyone says. I bet you have a serious friend whom everyone mocks, and one who's a bit tight, and a fat one, and one who's lucky with women, if a bit misogynist, and you're the funny one. I bet.

**Stories about my old job, of which I have loads and they are hilarious.** I get sent this one quite a lot, and it's not an absurd basis for comedy. *The Office* is rooted in it, most notably in Ricky Gervais and Stephen Merchant's observation that all offices are the same and they do all feature a cast of recognizable comic characters. But they took these characters as a starting point, and added Gervais's extraordinary monster David Brent. And then there's the legend of *Fawlty Towers*. Famously, it was turned down as the BBC had already done a sitcom about a funny hotel. But John Cleese and Connie Booth added to the formula an astonishing collection of grotesques, including a central character who both reflected our own desires and failings and made us feel superior to him.

The other point here is that people often think the setting is enough. If it's unusual, it's a show. This is a fair point: people do like to watch programmes about areas of life they don't know a lot about (although I can't think of a single example right now). But this is also why the offices of idle, snoring TV producers are often littered with unread scripts about the following subjects:

Life at a pirate radio station.

Life on a magazine.

Life on a rock magazine.

Ghosts.

Stand-up comedians.

An ad agency.

A model agency.

A behind-the-scenes-of a-TV-show sitcom.

And so on. These ideas turn up year on year, and they never seem to work. This is partly because of the comedy law that anything which is already beyond mockery can't be mocked. Therefore, rock music rarely works as comedy. How do you parody a world where people snort ants and blow cocaine up their own bottoms? Fashion is the same. How many fashion comedies (including the exception, the brilliant movie *Zoolander*) have done the scene where this year's new fashion is dressing like a tramp? It's been done in real life. Ad agencies are also crucibles for idiocy. The same applies to television: while I am no fan of the 'you can't do TV shows' rule, because it worked well enough for *Extras, 30 Rock*, and several others, it is difficult to send up a world where – and I pluck a random example from my own career – writers on a chat show are asked if they can somehow fit a ten foot tall arch in the shape of a vagina into the script as 'we've got one left over from our sex show.'

As for ghosts and stand-up comedians, I don't know if they're linked in any way but they both come up a lot and they both sometimes work, but I suspect they're both examples of an idea which manages to be simultaneously uncommon and overdone. Which is at least interesting.

**Mocking the dead format that is sitcom**.
Yeah, go to hell. Sitcom, like the novel, is
one of those formats which is still selling, still
popular and yet apparently dead. Perhaps it
has acquired a cult appeal like vinyl, or maybe
it's a ritualized form of entertainment like
the military recreation society. Perhaps it's a
ZOMBIE!

Most likely, it's alive, it's popular and it works.

Writing anything from a position of dislike is odd.
It can work, but if you don't like sitcoms (or dramas, or
musicals, or anything) you might be better off writing
something else. Lord knows what. The world, however,
is full of work by people who clearly hate the medium
they have chosen yet feel they can add something new
to it. You can see British romantic comedies written
by people who obviously loathe Richard Curtis films.
Musicals written by people with contempt for musicals.
Even the odd soap opera written by someone who feels
they could be doing better. Generally, if you feel you
should be on a higher level, you're almost certainly on a
higher level than you should be on. Oh, the neat irony.

Sitcom, then. Try and find a situation that's fresh.
Fresh doesn't mean absurd, it can just easily mean a
familiar object seen from an unfamiliar angle. And even
if you do set your show on a space station, or make it
about two teenage amoebas, you've still only set out a
corner of your stall. Who lives on this space station? (I
bet it's a sexy female officer and a gauche young man

officer. Single sex schools are the main reason British comedy can't do women.) What are these amoebas like? (I bet they enjoy fart gags and online porn. See above.)

The freshest sitcom takes that familiar object – the flatshare sitcom, the job sitcom, the relationship sitcom – and sees it from an unfamiliar angle. *Spaced* took the flatshare (aka I Have Never Had a Job or Experienced Life But I've Shared A Flat, aka The Most Boring And Overused Idea For A Sitcom) and gave it a mixture of surrealism, movie styling and an obsession with children's cinema. *Bluestone 42* took the job sitcom, made it an Army sitcom and set it in Afghanistan. *Modern Family* took the classic American family sitcom and made it, what's the word? Modern. Unless your amoeba sitcom is really about what it's like to be an amoeba, ask yourself what you get from the whole unicellular organism angle.

Sitcoms aren't just about their setting. *Father Ted*, perhaps to the dismay of its enemies, wasn't a satire on Catholicism. It may have mocked aspects of religion, Irish rural life, and the priesthood, but really it was a *Bugs Bunny* cartoon about a funny crook, a funny monster and a funny idiot. *Dad's Army* wasn't just about a platoon of Home Guard troops. It was about the reality of life during wartime for ordinary people, it was about a wide range of great comic characters – the mummy's boy, the spiv, the moaner, and many others – and it contained the best character reversal gag ever (the Captain is the middle-class character, the Sergeant the upper-class one. Tension and comedy).

If you have a new setting and great characters, so much the better. The drab teenage vampire boom of recent years has allowed shows like *Misfits* and *Being Human* to exist (if producers were postmen, your mail would always be two years late and they'd have copied it) using classic teen and outsider characters in ways that are both hilarious and moving. But instead of exploding your brain to think of A Setting That Hasn't Been Done (Heaven! A pet shop! Inside Michael Eavis!), you could take a setting that means something to you and explore it from a new angle. Maybe you're a new parent: what's it really like to be a parent now? Maybe you're a teacher: perhaps you're irked by the way comedy shows your job. New angles are just as good as new ideas.

Characters are trickier. One for the lads here: the amount of Sexy But Tough Women I see in scripts is depressing (it's just a fantasy rewrite of the Sexy But Not Tough Woman of the 1960s). Why not start writing women as characters before you write them as genders? You wouldn't start writing a male character with the words 'He's a man.' You'd start with 'He's a lazy git' or 'He's very angry.'

Characters don't need to be massively complex. The film, television and pop writer Geoffrey Deane (who we will be hearing from later) says that your character ought to be able to be described in one sentence. Try it, first with sitcom characters you like and then with your own creations. If you end up with 'Dan is a melancholy yet popular man whose love of Mary is only eclipsed by his love of *Star Wars*' ... well, please start again.

Mr. Deane's other fine bit of advice is that you should always know – as a writer and more importantly as a viewer – what a character would do in any situation. At once. What does Frasier Crane do when he sees a beautiful woman? What does Basil Fawlty do when he hears a posh voice? What does Jay from *The Inbetweeners* do in any situation? Again, try it with some famous characters and then with your own. If the answer is, 'I don't know', then go back to work.

And don't worry too much. If you're funny, your characters will be funny. Write bits of dialogue that typify them. Think of lines that only they could say (because if they constantly say stuff that's a) just smart one-liners or b) utterly bland, they're not characters, they're place-holders). You don't have to 'base them on people' or 'think of an outrageous character', just invent people who fit the situation, who will interact in a funny way with the other characters, and about whom you can write stories.

Stories are one of the hardest parts of writing comedy. For a start, they've all been done (one of the funniest episodes of *South Park* was called 'The Simpsons Already Did It', and was all about the difficulty of coming up with new ideas for an animated sitcom when... you get the picture). What your stories are completely depends on what kind of show you want to write: you can be minimalist and trivial, you can be emotional and wrought, you can be farcical and light... just be consistent, remember you're trying to create a world, and don't take the mickey out of your show (other people will do that for you) unless you really have to.

And that's it for sitcom. Don't bother with research until you've got your story, setting and characters (it's cart before the horse otherwise). Don't worry if you've no experience of the world you've set it in (*Blackadder* wasn't written by Elizabethans, *Steptoe and Son* wasn't written by rag and bone men, and so on). And ignore everything here if your idea is fantastic and original.

Oh, and if you send it to a producer and they haven't read it after a year, wait till they've gone home and firebomb their office. They clearly don't need it.

## Chapter Six
# Films

Or movies. It doesn't matter. Making a film in the United Kingdom is a strange business; for a start, it's one of the few areas of British life other than passport control where you get to use the phrase 'the United Kingdom'. But it's also a reflection of the UK's very odd position in the world; this country is either a force to be reckoned with as a movie-making nation, or it's a cinematic backwater. Other countries (by which we mean 'other countries who aren't America') seem to have no difficulty producing films. Everyone from France to Korea, from India to Australia, has an indigenous and individual film industry, producing and releasing movies which reflect the tastes of the population but also have a saleable worldwide identity. Meanwhile in the UK, it often feels that we make two kinds of films: Cockney gangster retreads in the Guy Ritchie/Quentin Tarantino tradition, or posh romcoms in a Richard Curtis style.

Obviously this isn't entirely true (although in many ways, it is entirely true), but making a film in Britain is not easy. So instead of parroting Robert McKee and other experts on writing a hit film script, I thought I'd hand you over to a couple of friends of mine. Geoffrey Deane is a comedy writer of long-standing who's written several hit British sitcoms and also some comedy films, most notably *Kinky Boots*, which recently became a successful Broadway Musical (which seems apt, as Geoff began his career during punk as one of the wittier song-writers of the era). I've know Geoff for a very long time and can testify that he is as warm and funny as he is terrifying, and he is quite terrifying.

By slight contrast, Michael Knowles is a film producer based in the North of England. He's also warm and funny, and not terrifying at all. Mike and I are currently working on a couple of projects, one of which is a comedy film, and the other an extension of *Snodgrass*, a Sky Arts *Playhouse* one-off which we're hoping to develop into a full-length feature. Mike has produced several films, including the brilliant *A Boy Called Dad*, with Ian Hart.

But first, let's hear from Geoff Deane.

**DQ: You've written TV and cinema. What are the main differences for a writer between a TV script and a film script?**

GD: In TV the standing of the director and writer is inverted. So you have a better shot at getting what you want on screen. In the US they take that to the next level and TV writers go on to become show runners and producers. That's why American dramas and comedies are often so good and can go on for so long. The writers are in charge – of other writers. And it works. Amazing. Who'd have thought? The people that came up with the show and write the show actually know best.

There's been a long-term drift of top writers from movies to TV in the US. Films are now the place to find two giant robots from outer space battering each other so they can sell you shit for your games console. TV has *Breaking Bad* and *Parks & Recreation*. Spot the difference.

## What should be in every script?

The very best professional endeavour you are capable of at that point in time. Show respect to your craft and the people who are going to read your work. See, I can be serious. I get very intolerant of young erstwhile writers who want to break into movies or TV. I look at their work and it's not even set out properly and it's 250 pages long. You may as well write I KNOW FUCK ALL on the title page. Do your research, put the hours in, don't look a mug. The first sitcom I ever wrote was formatted perfectly, the correct length, with the right amount of characters, scenes and story lines. Same with my first movie script. And this was in the days before the internet, where everything is now so easily within one's grasp. My work may not have actually been any good but it showed I'd done my homework.

## How valuable is an original idea?

True originality is the single biggest disadvantage I can think of for any script. People always tell you they're looking for something original. But they're not. And you know what? They're right. There's enough risks commensurate with film-making without looking for new ones all the time. Look at it like this. If you went to see Ford and told them you'd invented an engine that runs on tropical fish they'd show you the door, no matter how impressive your pitch. They are not in the fish engine business. But tell them you've refined a standard engine so that it runs better and more economically and they'll phone through for coffee and doughnuts. Most films are new takes on things you have seen before. That is something an industry can do.

When I was writing *Kinky Boots* all I heard from the producers were *The Full Monty* and *Calendar Girls*. Two rare British films which made money. It was their daily mantra. They even gave me scenes to put in lifted from them which made little sense in the context of my film. And all I wanted to write about was a tranny and high-quality footwear. If you look back at the posters and publicity material for the film, Lola (said tranny) was neither seen nor mentioned. This was meant to be a film about resilient Brits triumphing against adversity by doing something marginally risqué, not a film about cross-dressing. That aspect was too original so it was hidden from the public. When it was adapted for the stage show the Broadway producers had no such reservations. They came from a different culture with different mores. The all-singing, all-dancing tranny *Kinky Boots* picked up six Tony Awards and has been a huge success. So this is not just an anecdote about originality. It's also one about producers.

### How much of a script when finally filmed is yours?

To quote the late Stevie Marriott, all or nothing. It's not your call. This medium is all about the director. He's higher up the pecking order and it's his call, despite the fact that it's your idea that you've been nurturing for the last five years and have poured your heart and a lifetime of professional experience into. He made a half decent short a few years back so he knows best.

### What are the pros and cons of: directors?

See above. I hear tell that there are directors who can elevate your work to a different level. Personally I'm happy with one that can shoot the script and keep the boom out of shot. Most screenwriters that I know love movies and are very well versed in moviemaking. When I write a scene I know what actors I want to play the characters, how the set should be dressed and what music, if any, should be playing. I write from a deeply filmic perspective, as do most of my colleagues. It's a little bit mental that these decisions are usually left to the director and you aren't even consulted.

**Pros and cons of: actors.**

I like actors. They're bonkers, talented and deal with a lot of rejection. So we have common ground. I don't like it when they're difficult. That encroaches on my territory.

**Pros and cons of: producers.**

A good producer gets your film made. A great one makes it better than you dared dream and the process enjoyable. The worst are the stuff of nightmares. I have had the very spark of life sucked from my soul in years of development meetings with these guys. Do you want to hear about the producer who rewrote part of my script and then bollocked me for something he'd actually written? You couldn't make it up. Well, you could but they'd give you notes and want it changed anyway.

**Pros and cons of: writers.**

We are the best. Intelligent, creative people whose personalities have been distorted out of all proportion due to years of having the shit kicked out of them and sporadic flirtations with success. Fantastic company especially when there's booze involved. The collective noun for a group of writers gathered together is a KVETCH.

**Is there one story that sums up the process of trying to get a film made?**

You know the fable about the cripple trying to make his way up a steep hill smeared with chicken fat, with a rucksack full of bowling balls strapped to his back and a bottle of cold piss for sustenance? That.

**Why are there so few British films?**

If I was the kind of person who used phrases like 'Don't get me started', now would be a good time. In simple terms you have to find a lot of money to make a British movie, say somewhere between one and fourteen million squids. That is money which statistically speaking you are almost guaranteed not to make back. So it is not an incredibly attractive proposition to investors. Where it gets interesting is *why* our films lose dough, because when it comes to above-the-line talent we can pretty much swing dicks with the best of them. But we are operating within a system where the odds are stacked against us immeasurably. We are swamped by American movies. They each cost around ten to twenty times more than our films, feature the world's biggest stars, and have huge budgets to promote them. Whereas you've been sweating blood to find the four million you wanted to make your film 'properly' and have been compromising from day one. It's like Port Vale being drawn against Real Madrid. Should you be one of the fortunate few to cross the finishing line with a completed film you then have to get it noticed and seen. We work with minuscule promotional budgets or none at all. And our commercial cinema chains are basically buildings for showing American movies.

Some years back I wrote a movie called *It's a Boy Girl Thing*. A high school body swap movie. The producers were Rocket, Sir Elton John's company. A great outfit who have got their shit together better than most. The budget was around eight mill. We'd had some of the usual problems, like the phone call at 3am saying 'You know the big house party scenes in the middle of the movie? They're not going to happen. Can you give us something which does the same job but with just two boys walking down the street?' We got through that. And we got our film made. Not perfectly by any means. But it had such a strong commercial premise that still held up. Still does. It was released at the same time as *Night at the Museum*. With Ben Stiller, Robin Williams, Owen Wilson and Paul Rudd as well as Steve Coogan and Ricky Gervais. That cost around $120 mill and was promoted massively. We had some posters up in bus shelters. I wanted to take my kids to see *Boy Girl Thing* at the local Odeon so I checked the listings. On that day there were over twenty screenings of *Night at the Museum* to choose from. There were three of my film. So you're never in with a real shout.

## Why are British films often not as good as European or Asian films?

Because of the above, the UK film business is one desperate, mad scramble to reach the finishing line. That's not a culture conducive to great film-making. The main drive goes into finding the money to make the movie rather than making a great movie. And the people that succeed in getting their films made are those best positioned to raise money, not those that can make the best films. It's a big pile of wrong from bottom to top, stacked high. A few years ago Dexter Fletcher wrote and directed his first movie, *Wild Bill*. It had no big stars and was made for only 700K. But it was a great little film, a miracle on that budget. A moving, compelling story, elegantly constructed. It received very little push and what marketing there was did it no favours. There was a terrible poster. All tough-looking geezers with two clenched fists to the fore. It gave you no clue of the huge amount of heart that lay within. The film didn't hit many screens and made back only 60K. That in a nutshell is everything wrong with our business.

European countries can and do make great films (and TV) which are both a bonus to their culture and good business. Look at Scandinavia. It's all about having a supportive infrastructure competently administrated. But we are as far from that as we have ever been. And because of that messy, vaguely glamorous terrain we operate in, the business attracts a lot of idiots who clog up the works. A confederacy of the utterly clueless. Jackie Mason once said that he's always meeting guys that call themselves producers but all they ever produce are business cards. That's my life, that is.

## What, if any, are the advantages of working in the UK?

You speak the language and it's convenient for seeing the kids.

## Are screenwriting courses any use?

They can be, I guess. I was already up and running when I suddenly realised I'd never had any formal training as a writer. So I did the Robert McKee course. It was okay. But in truth just a very drawn out version of what I'd learned from watching *Cheers* all those years ago. John Cleese was in the class and he'd already written *A Fish Called Wanda* so I felt in good company. But I think McKee is a clever man. All he ever wrote was one episode of *Spenser: For Hire* and I paid him money. That's talent.

All writers need an intimate understanding of structure and disciplines. But they should be at your disposal, not you at theirs. The problem with relentlessly following formula is that it produces clichés. The first writer that had a cop's boss lean on him to make solving the case even more difficult had a great idea. 10,000 films later it's meaningless. It doesn't up the ante, it just says lazy writing.

**What is a common waste of time for a film writer?**

Sadly, writing films. Like many good writers my best work remains on my hard drive.

**Are you astonishingly rich?**

Yes. My house is built onto a vast cave of gold. Nah. Of course not. Not even close.

**After years as a writer, you still seem enthusiastic about your job. What keeps you going?**

The writing. It's just what I do. I am happy when I do something good or make myself laugh.

\* \* \*

I have nothing to add to the above except that everything I know about structure, character and plot I learned from Geoff, and everything I don't know about those things I learned from books.

Geoff does retain enthusiasm and love for his work, even if it is sometimes a little buried. Mike Knowles, on the other hand, is full of *joie de vivre* even on the bleakest days:

**DQ: Describe yourself.**

MK: I am a dad, songwriter and creative film and TV producer.

## What do you do?

I develop, package and finance scripts. I always find as a producer you have to make the film in your head or on paper before it is made in actuality. The templates for this are the script, sales pack, budget, schedule etc. With those elements you should be able to tell investors (and the creative team) etc. how you are making a film creatively, what it will look like and when and how money will be spent (and with sales estimates what return it might make).

## What is a film producer? How does it differ from other kinds of producer?

You earn less money! It seems that most producers I meet already have some money or are lawyers. Increasingly it is almost impossible for producers and companies to work solely in film. However in terms of look and 'feel' on screen I approach each project the same way. I would have said five years ago the scope, vision and power of a film was different to now. However there is now a huge crossover and the difference is often how the work is financed and transmitted.

There was and is also a snobbery from film to TV. However there is a huge crossover between top-end TV and film (certainly within British film)! Television is changing in terms of what is produced for it.

**Films are said to be collaborations. Apart from the obvious, what is the place of a writer in a film, from idea to release?**

For me the writer is the centre of the creative development of a film – other people may be involved (most notably a director or myself) but the writers are the beating core.

**How do writers approach films in your experience?**

It depends on their backgrounds and what they have worked on previously. The best ones I have worked with are prepared to try ideas out knowing that it may be a long process (but that I will be working as hard as them in trying to get the project off the ground). Buying into this collaboration between the writer and producer is important for me.

**What do you look for in a script?**

I should say something that will excite the public and make me loads of money. However as I usually end up working on a film for five to seven years (if it gets made!) any script would have to move me, make me laugh or get a response. I have to know I will like it five years from the original read.

**What do you look for in a writer?**

I love working with writers who welcome input and who don't have to have a cuddle or reassurance every time a comma is changed. So I would say writers who are not precious and who are passionate about their craft but are keen to collaborate with a producer who will flog his guts out to try to get the film made. A sense of humour is also essential as it is a long and difficult process.

## How do you think a film writer might differ from a TV or other writer?

I think it is harder and harder (apart from the top feature writers perhaps) to work solely as a film writer in the UK. So in that case a British feature writer might have a smaller house than his TV colleague! And emerging film writers will probably initially be dependent of BFI, Creative England subsidy and so forth.

## Film scripts change all the time; does this mean a writer has to be adaptable?

A writer definitely has to be adaptable. Scripts change, financiers change, times change, actors change. All this will impact upon a script and what is required of the writer.

## When do you want a writer to become involved in a film? And when are they not needed?

Writers are all always needed! Obviously when shooting a film there isn't much that can be done but I have enjoyed the writer/producer relationship most when I have been able to continue the collaboration from development to the edit. If you can develop that relationship in the development process it is possible to carry through and be a true team effort.

## If I was eighteen and thought I could write better films than the ones I've seen, what should I do?

If you think you can write you definitely should try writing and learn by your mistakes and failures. I met Anthony Burgess when I was a teenager and he described writing as akin to a muscle that needs to be exercised regularly – so start exercising.

It is also important (and I say this reluctantly) to hound producers. However it may help if you sleep with someone at the BBC or Film4 or the BFI (joking – you probably don't have to sleep with them).

## Is there any point being a film writer in Britain?

There definitely is a real point in being a film writer in the UK. However you should be realistic in that it is very competitive out there and there are lots of knocks. Also I think it is probably quite difficult to be solely a film writer (and you may need jobs not in the media industry to support this). I think perhaps the writer is more central to television than to film (though for me there isn't a huge difference between the two media).

\* \* \*

And there you have it, two people who make and have made movies. It all sounds a bit cloudy with occasional flashes of sun. Then again, I've always found the movie business more accommodating than television, perhaps because of the lack of hoops. I'm forming a theory here, about hoops; the more hoops you have to jump through to get your project made, the less fun and the less worthwhile it will be. Not always – but when the process of amending and altering your work at the suggestion of others is pleasant and rewarding, we call that process 'collaboration.' When that process is horrible and dirtying, we call it 'jumping through hoops.' And lots of other, less nice names. There are so many stories about movies which have been altered beyond recognition in the process of being produced – actors changed from fat to thin, settings changed from Africa to the Moon, thrillers to romance and so on (if you have a mo, look up the story of the movie *Knight and Day* sometime; it's very funny, unless you worked on it). And often this process is necessary; I've read early drafts of films as diverse as *The Full Monty* and *American Beauty* and in those instances the redrafting process was a good thing.

Film is full of hoops, of course; but often it's less stultifying than dealing with broadcasters, whose requirements – often divorced from mere money-making – can be an assault course for second-guessers, in which committees lie in wait with guidelines designed to protect people who couldn't care less if they're offended or not. And so on.

And then there's short films. My producer and director colleague John Panton has written a blog under his prodco name of MeatBingo about the magical process of making a film from nothing, using only goodwill, talent and, of all things, Twitter. His point is that anything is possible, and it's a good point. Our last short film began as a pop video that the client didn't like. We reworked it, added a voice-over and turned it into a sinister art film. It then won a European film festival prize. As technology makes possible cheap movies that couldn't have been made for less than a million dollars twenty years ago, as the net enables anyone to talk to anyone about collaborating (just say yes), and as the entertainment industry reels like a drunk man who keeps having his shoulder tapped by ghosts, the goalposts aren't so much moving as dancing to the rhythm of *The Guns of Navarone*.

Short version of the last three paragraphs; if you want to make films, do so. Don't mess about with telly and so forth. Make friends, learn stuff, make films.

## Chapter Seven
# Writing a Script and So On

Scripts come in all shapes and (you're ahead of me, I can tell) sizes. As I've hinted, formatting can be important (movie scripts generally have to be formatted in the accepted style) but quite often it doesn't matter that much. I write radio scripts like this:

CROWD NOISE

DAVID
I'm dancing and singing in Brighton in 1981 –

BUCKS FIZZ LIVE MAKING YOUR MIND UP

DAVID
and a man's just pulled my skirt off! Giggle!

CROWD OO

DAVID
And I'm spitting fire in Athens in 2006! Roar!

LORDI SONG – FX FLAMETHROWER

FLAMES. SCREAMING

And the producer will put it into the correct format for the production team. But then, we know each other. I've worked with presenters who write their own scripts, full of misspellings, long directions, in-jokes and insults, and if you're working on an established show with a sympathetic team, it doesn't matter that much. But if you're a new writer, or at least one unknown to the people you're working with, it's basic good manners if nothing else to present your work in a coherent manner.

The central plank of script-writing is this: One page equals one minute. Roughly speaking, that is. And no matter how you crop your margins or extend your footers, no matter how many sound effects or directions you put in, your page will come in at a minute long. If it doesn't, that's because you've been told a script is thirty or sixty pages long and, like Cinderella's ugly sisters, you've chopped off appendages to make it fit. Don't. Don't fit your verbiage in by using tiny typeface or make your lack of words reach up with your enormous spacing. Write what looks normal. If you don't know what looks normal, go online and look at scripts.

Scripts are of course all what we industry insiders call 'different lengths.' But once you know that one page equals one minute (roughly speaking), you can work out how long your script is going to be. So a UK sitcom script for the BBC would be thirty pages, while a non-BBC script would be twenty-three pages. A short Radio 4 script would be fifteen pages. A radio or TV documentary might be thirty or sixty pages. And so on. This might sound basic (it is basic) but it's surprising how often people just sort of hope their script will be the right length. Please remember that there is nothing more depressing for a reader than a pdf or a printed document that looks like it will never, ever end.

Film scripts have their own rules, too. You'd really be doing the right thing if you invested in a screen-writing program. I use Final Draft. It gives you options for different kinds of script format and, once you've mastered its basic elements, it does most of the work for you. There are other brands, and again a quick online search will tell you which of your favourite writers uses what kind of program. Yes, they're not cheap but then you want to do this for a living, don't you?

Films are also different lengths. A comedy is shorter, being generally 91–100 minutes long. (The best comedies are 106 minutes long.) A feature can be any length; if it has action and fighting, particularly between superheroes, it can be almost three hours. Two hours is fine, though; if it takes you more than that to tell a story, you are either rambling or trying to sell action figures. Then there are short films, of which I have written several (Google 'Lot 13 MeatBingo' some time). A short film is not a film that isn't very long. It's a specific kind of film, just as a short story is a specific kind of story. It has its own rules, its own styles, and its own limits – one of which is that it's rarely less than two minutes and more than eight minutes long. If your 'short film' script is twenty or forty or even sixty minutes long, it's not a short film. It's probably an unfinished long film and you should keep working at it.

(An aside on short films; they are a great, cheapish way to learn how to make movies. As well as that, they're a fantastic genre in themselves, where you can be atmospheric, experimental, or daft, largely because those qualities work in short bursts, whereas they can be dull or annoying over two hours. They're also a good way to publicise your abilities.)

I won't spend much time here on the mechanics of laying out a script, but I will address one particular bugbear: over-fulsome directions. Directions are a minefield for new writers – you want to make everything plain for the reader but you also run the risk of overwhelming the script with detail. Just as footnotes turn a reference book into a boot-sucking slurry of verbal molasses (and they're not as funny in comedy books as comedy book writers think they are, either)[2], so directions in a script can sound like you've lost your <u>mind on the first</u> page. Which is not ideal.

2   Footnotes are really annoying. See?

Here's the sort of thing I mean:

INT. TRAVEL AGENT – DAY

JASON, a YOUNG MAN in his 20s – maybe 23-24, although he could pass for younger, and indeed often gets carded – is sitting at the COMPUTER, his JACKET draped over a SWIVEL CHAIR.

The TRAVEL AGENT'S OFFICE is decorated with a variety of POSTERS, each depicting various EXOTIC LOCATIONS. There are MODEL AIR LINERS on the counter, all a bit DUSTY. And there is a MODEL of an AIR INDIA LOGO FIGURE, the little man who looks slightly like MARIO in a turban.

The SHOP BELL dings. JASON sighs, turns off the game of WORLD OF WARCRAFT he is playing, and turns to face –

A WOMAN in her early 50s/late 40s. She is wearing a HAWAIIAN SHIRT, a SOMBRERO, and SUNGLASSES. She has a STUFFED DONKEY under one arm and a PINATA under the other.

WOMAN (in SPANISH ACCENT)
Bon jour! Aloha! Caramba!

Bit busy, innit? The point of directions is to convey essential information. Not all the above information needs to be there (and a lot of it will change before filming anyway). In this case, the info you don't need would be the overly detailed ages of the characters and most of the description of the travel agency. (We also don't need the name of the game Jason is playing.) What we should keep, apart from the names and rough ages of the characters, would be the information that tells us this is a rundown office, not a brand new one, and arguably the description of the woman. Clearly the writer is trying to tell us that she is either mad or obsessed with the idea of being a tourist, and as this adds something new to the otherwise predictable nature of a scene where someone goes into a travel agency, this is worth keeping.

That doesn't mean, of course, you should go the other way:

INT. OFFICE – DAY

JASON is working. A WOMAN comes in.

WOMAN
Hello.

This conveys so little as to be worthless. But it's your call. You may want to reveal information in dialogue later, or to bring in the classic comedy device:

PULL BACK TO REVEAL

But this should always be used sparingly, if at all. It's a tricky one (not that tricky, mind); you want the script to accurately reflect what the viewer would see, but at the same time you can't literally show that, so you have to create a kind of simulacrum of what the viewer would see. Either way, don't over- or under-describe.

Most other script points are not for us here. There are books, hell, civilizations devoted to explaining how script structure works. Some writers love talking in terms of three-act structure, story arcs and beats; some really hate it. I would say that knowledge of and the ability to break story down into its component parts is incredibly useful, just as knowing how a car is put together is clearly a good way to start making a car. That said, it's arguably a brake on the imagination when you use conventional story-writing plans every step of your way. As someone said, the problem with a lot of Hollywood movies is that, if a character picks up a violin and plays it, you know for sure that their ability to play the violin is going to be essential to the plot later on in the story (whereas if it's an old-fashioned art movie, it's probably because violins sound nice).

I'm concerned here with making sure that we understand certain aspects of what a script is and what it is not. What it is not is the finished item. A script is not the film, or the show. It can be – it can be recorded or filmed verbatim and it can be brilliant. (By the way, if you buy a 'shooting script' in book form, be careful – it's often just a transcript of the finished film or play, not the script as it evolved through rehearsal and rewrites. You should go online and buy earlier drafts; like the deleted scenes and director's commentaries on a DVD, they're a lot more useful to someone trying to improve their writing, because they show the workings, as it were.) That's not to say that a script is, as the late Peter Wyngarde once told a director we were working with, 'just a guide for the actors.' A script is more than the skeleton of a film or show, it's the muscle and flesh and hair and eyes, and arguably the shoes and trousers too. But it's not the finished product.

If you've ever worked with an obsessive or a perfectionist, you will know that they are generally convinced that there is a sort of Holy Grail version of a script, a version of the story in which every line, every direction and every moment cannot be improved upon. And maybe that's the case. Certainly there are films and shows where it would be immensely difficult to imagine a better version. However, these are rare, and an examination of earlier drafts or deleted scenes may well show that some of the changes made here and there before filming or recording were just as good or better.

A final draft of a script is not final because it is the complete, most perfect version of that script. It is final because – and only because – it is the one that got filmed. Sometimes this isn't very good (you may recall the US TV shows hastily put together after the writers' strike a few years back, some of which were quite undercooked) but most of the time, if the people involved are any good, it's great. For proof of this, look at the endless Director's Cuts of various movies, or the embarrassing 'improvements' George Lucas has made to the original *Star Wars* films; they may well be closer to what was in somebody's head, but they are actually worse than the original, imperfect versions. The final version is the final version, and that is, literally, an end to it.

So your script will go on, and go round, and if you're unlucky, go under. I've worked on scripts where location, character and story have changed constantly, like that broomstick whose head and stick kept being replaced, until the only element remaining is the central character. I've seen scripts retain one idea or even one joke, and I've seen scripts that started out full of laughter and optimism, only to sink wordlessly into chaos a few weeks later. The sole constant in your script is likely to be you, so keep going; they hired you because they like your writing, and unless you become a sudden convert to concrete poetry or freestyle rapping halfway through, that will remain a constant.

Flexibility, by the way, is a tricky one also. It's for you to decide whether you should give in and make your hero a blonde-haired, muscular jock instead of the spotty nerd you envisaged. But you should also remember that, just because someone who makes programmes for money is asking you to change something, it doesn't necessarily mean they are doing so for sinister means. They might be right, and having a hero who's a sort of invisible jelly could be hard to film. They might be right, and calling your villain Mickey Mouseface could cause legal difficulties. And they might be right about your female lead being appallingly written. They might also be wrong, but conceding one point to make them feel good so they'll concede to you on another, more important issue could be the way to go here. It's really up to you; as Kenny Rogers sang in Don Schlitz's 'The Gambler', you got to know when to hold 'em, and when to fold 'em.

Another thing about scripts is that they are calling cards. You might not have written anything somebody has made, but you have, if you've got a script you're pleased with, got something you can use to say to people, this is what I can do. And yes, scripts do end up mouldering in piles in rooms where no one goes, but sometimes they get read. My fantastic agent Kate Haldane routinely sends out scripts I wrote for shows that didn't get made because they illustrate not just that I can write but what I can write and how I write it.

(I haven't really touched on agents in this book because, while they're a big part of writing, getting an agent is something you'll have to work on yourself. My brief tip as ever is look at writers you admire and see who their agents are. Write or email asking to send that agent some stuff. And be politely persistent. It's hard to get an agent but if you're lucky, you'll find one who'll spot your potential.)

Oh! Pitch documents. Because writing is still not just the process of getting ideas you've written down onto film, but also the process of making people understand just what it is you want to do. (An aside; after writing a pitch document for a radio show where we kept saying, 'This is not an audience show,' we had our idea rejected for being… an audience show. The producer concerned had skimmed the pitch and the words 'audience show' had leapt out at them. So be careful how you phrase everything.) When you're working out the early stages of your brilliant robot ballet, or your sitcom about twin rabbis, or your silent war movie, you should also be working out how to explain it.

When I write a pitch, also known as a treatment, I do this.

1. I put the title of the show down – THE BAD BROTHER.

2. Then I write one or two lines describing the show: 'Alan comes home one night to find his brother Calum has moved back in. Only problem is, Calum's wanted for fraud in fourteen countries.'

3. Next I'll expand that description – the show is a comedy, it's six thirty-minute episodes, it's filmed in front of an audience, and it's an exploration of family ties and how they react

to strain. Only I'll say it in a more interesting and funny way.

4. Then I'll do a list of characters – Alan, the meek but likeable hero. Calum, the rude but even more likable brother. Lisa, the long-suffering girlfriend who wants Calum out. Mister Boss, Alan's terrifying boss. Auntie Mrs Funny, a comical neighbour. And if I can think of any, I'll suggest well-known actors to play these roles – not because I can get them, but because commissioners find it easier to visualize characters if they can see a famous person's face in their head.

5. And I'll round it up with six short episode summaries – EPISODE THREE : Alan wants to buy a sensible car, but Calum makes him get a Porsche. Meanwhile Mister Boss wants Alan to drink a pint of concrete for Sport Relief.

Hey, I'd watch it.

Some other areas where different kinds of scripts prevail, briefly.

A **radio script** can, as I say, be formatted quite loosely but the important thing to remember here – and I realise as I type this how uncomplex a thought it is – is that your script is utterly sound-based. You can, if you wish, just transcribe your TV idea or your novel but it's best to remember that radio isn't the second choice after television, but a completely different and exciting way of presenting ideas. On radio you can do anything, your budgets are tiny but the universe, not just the world, is your oyster, and you can move from outer space to Jane Austen's England to inside a frog's mind within seconds. (Despite this, when Jane Bussmann and I wrote an effect direction in a script for 'a medieval farm on a spaceship', the radio producer involved said, 'It's impossible!' It wasn't impossible.) You can shift from dialogue to interior monologue to pure sound, and in this respect, oddly, radio resembles cinema (both, I suppose, being rooted in one sense, whether it's sound or vision). So if you're adapting your novel, add sound and sound effects. And if you're reworking your TV script, remember that this:

INT. TRAVEL AGENT – DAY

JASON, a YOUNG MAN in his 20s – maybe 23-24, although he could pass for younger, and indeed often gets carded – is sitting at the COMPUTER, his JACKET draped over a SWIVEL CHAIR.

is completely inaudible. So read radio scripts and learn the language of radio.

**Sketches**, radio or otherwise, are odd things. It took me years to learn how to write them, because I had no idea what a sketch was. Even with the crutch of writing for puppet caricatures of famous people, I couldn't think of an angle or a way in (or out – for years people struggled with punchlines for sketches, until Spike Milligan got bored and abolished them). In the end I realised that the best sketches are just ideas. Forget puns, forget punchlines and above all forget

## PULL BACK TO REVEAL

A good sketch is just a good idea. Monty Python's Parrot Sketch, while overfamiliar to generations, is really a sketch about a sarcastic man who won't stop mocking his victim. With the addition of John Cleese's silly voice and some inspired variations on the idea of death visiting a parrot, as well as Michael Palin's perfectly nonchalant foil, it's brilliant. Eddie Izzard's great routine about Darth Vader visiting the canteen on the Death Star has one central comic idea: a terrible creature doing something mundane. French and Saunders' sketch about one teenage girl wrongly explaining sex to her friend is another great central idea: the one-upmanship of the ignorant over the more ignorant (YouTube it, do). If you have an idea, and it's funny, you have a sketch. It can be a character, a phrase or a juxtaposition; either way, one idea is all you need.

**Comics!** I've written a strip with Savage Pencil called *Louis Wain* in Alan Moore's 'Dodgem Logic' and I've also written my first complete comic with Shaky Kane, a one-off called *That's Because You're A Robot* (and I wrote some Harry Hill storylines for, yes, *The Dandy*). There are, as far as I know, no official templates for comic-writing, but I just copied Moore's scripts for Dave Gibbons on *Watchmen*. Some artists like to be told what to draw in detail, others like a lot of leeway, but generally as a writer you'll work out a balance with the artist. It's surprising how few words you'll use. Well, I suppose it's not that surprising.

**Everything else** is a variation on one or other of the above. So that's some general stuff about putting a script together. The content, as ever, is up to you or your overlords. Now I'd like to talk about the collaborative process, using as examples one or two shows I've worked on.

When you start writing you will submit stuff. There are always radio shows or TV shows who will take unsolicited material if it's good enough. If it's not good enough, boo hoo. Write some more until it is good enough. People may be rejecting your work because they're idiots, but it still doesn't hurt you to keep writing until you find a friend. And if you really thought your old stuff was good, you can look at it again and, if you find you were right, get it made now you're better known (this was, as I may have said, the genesis of my short film *Lot 13*).

Sketch shows are useful for getting your name around, as they will eventually get you In The Room. The Room is not the American Writers' Room, where genius one-liners fly like bullets, but a different Room. It may be on a panel game, a chat show, a clip show, or a combination of lots of different things (I am currently about to start work script-editing a clip show hosted by an impressionist). When you're starting out, being in The Room is great; you meet other writers, you get direct contact with the Talent (the people you're writing for) and you meet people like producers and runners. Important! Be nice to everyone. Runners grow up fast and become producers themselves or commissioners, and if they liked you three years ago and thought you were funny, they might hire you. If they remember you as the dipstick who kept complaining about the coffee you brought them, they won't hire you. Also, just be nice to people. What's wrong with you?

The Room is often an aggressive place, being full generally of men who are intelligent and who must perforce spend their time writing, essentially, putdowns (very few jokes are positive, after all). It can be a depressing place if your sense of humour is a whimsical and delicate one. It can be a horrible place if everyone is male. And it can be great. I spent nearly a decade as a 'programme associate' (writer) on *Harry Hill's TV Burp* and everyone, without fail, from producer and star downwards was incredibly lovely.

Mention of *TV Burp* reminds me I was going to talk about shows I've worked on and the processes therein. They are, generally, very different. *TV Burp*, being clip-led, meant we all had to watch decades of TV, some of it almost bearable, to find sight gags, comic moments and, most importantly, moments in shows for Harry to spin out into floppy-collared flights of brilliance. It was quite hard to keep up, but after a decade we found it easier, a bit, in that we had gone from saying, 'I think this clock looks a bit like a face, if you ignore the fact it doesn't have a nose' and 'The animal at the back of this shot looks as though it has amazingly long legs' to 'One of these,' 'One of those' and 'Window goat on *Emmerdale*.'

*TV Burp* had, has and will have its imitators, but sometimes a show will only work with its central figure. Harry Hill's a comedian, not a presenter, and without him and his peculiar humour, the show wouldn't work. Similarly, one of the most underrated shows I wrote for, *Saturday Zoo*, was reliant on its central figure being Jonathan Ross. The show combined the sketch and music and stand-up format of *Saturday Night Live* with Jonathan's own interview style. It introduced the world to Mark Thomas and Steve Coogan (as Paul Calf), it had great music and big names, but the public didn't quite go for it. As a writing experience, though, it was extraordinary, because the writers were given loose ideas to work up for those big names, and The Room was for once thrilling (please check out our best moment on YouTube, Christopher Walken reading *The Three Little Pigs*).

At the same time, bizarrely, I was writing with Steven Wells on *The Day Today*. More Steve Coogan (this time as Alan Partridge) as well as never-used *Saturday Zoo* cast Patrick Marber, Rebecca Front, plus Doon Mackichan, Peter Baynham and Chris Morris. Armando Iannucci and Chris ran the show to a large extent between themselves, which meant the show was very directionful – that is, we'd all work on similar ideas and the results would be pooled.

On both *Saturday Zoo* and *The Day Today*, very different shows in tone and style, there was the additional element, new to me, of performer-written material. Previously, everything I'd worked on had been with actors. Now I was working with people like Simon Day and John Thomson, or Patrick Marber and Chris Morris, who wrote their own scripts and performed them. This is why I do sometimes suggest to people that if you can perform, do. Unless of course all your ideas are about angry Northern pensioners and you're a young Guernsey lad.

The top-down form of working on a show, where the producer/presenter generates ideas with a small core team and farms them out was also a large part of the process on Chris Morris' *Brass Eye* and, to some extent, the *jam* and *Blue Jam* series, but it was an informal process and Jane Bussmann and I always felt encouraged to come up with horrific ideas of our own.

Jane and I worked on our own and with the cast on *Smack The Pony*, a classic sketch show. I'm still very happy we wrote a sketch with Sally Phillips, about a hostage chained to a radiator. We also worked on *The Fast Show*, which was fun as we'd write a batch of sketches, send them in, and later get a very gruff phone call from Paul Whitehouse telling us to write four more.

In the 21st century, I've worked on a very strange variety of shows, from *Jimmy's Food Factory* (friend of Jamie Oliver explains how modern food is made) to *Coach Trip* (where I had to narrate complex and tongue-breaking paragraphs written by committee). I came in at the end of *The Thick of It*, and I've co-written episodes of *Veep* (shows on which The Room is a huge virtual soup where ideas lurk like croutons).

And so it goes on, different shows and different Rooms. Some people want light, frothy comedy, and some want dark, aggressive comedy. Some people want you to do all the work and some people won't let you do any. If you contribute to sketch shows, you don't get much money or credit, but nobody minds if you fail. If you're writing your own show, every episode is a terrible test of character.

In the end, though, whatever you write, it'll be a script. So you'd better write one.

### Chapter Eight
# Plays

'The only thing I get from the theatre is a sore arse,' John Lennon told Joe Orton, who may have read other layers into that somewhat Puritan statement. I tend to sympathise with Lennon. I am aware that without plays, we wouldn't have any form of scripted drama or comedy; that plays (particularly those of Shakespeare, you know) have enriched our lives and our vocabularies; and that theatre is both cultural heritage and cultural future.

That said, I don't really go to the theatre. Some people don't like musicals because they can't accept that a person might just break off talking and burst into song. I find it weird to see a bunch of people in make-up standing on a platform and shouting at each other. I also wonder why, in an age when story-telling in films and television is often streamlined and beautifully plotted, plays seem so rambling. Scenes don't advance the plot, characters bang on about nothing, and stories which wouldn't trouble a thirty minute episode of *Emmerdale* go on and on for three hours. The arse is indeed severely tested.

So I thought it would be a bit unfair to you, the reader, who might want to write a play, to pretend that I knew anything about the theatre. I asked two people to assist me. The first is playwright Tanika Gupta, MBE, who describes herself as someone who writes 'plays for the stage mainly but I also write dramas for radio and film. I used to write a lot for television as well but not so much these days.' During the last fifteen years Tanika has written over twenty stage plays that have been produced at theatres including the Royal Court, National Theatre, Young Vic, and for the Royal Shakespeare Company. She's also written thirty radio plays for the BBC.

**DQ: What did you like about theatre?**

TG: I love the theatre because it's LIVE! I have always enjoyed going to the theatre because I like the smell and atmosphere of it. I like being able to see actors up close and think there's a certain magical quality to a night at the theatre. I like straight plays as well as musicals; Shakespeare as well as new plays, but most of all I enjoy watching live performances and seeing stories unfold. I also like the fact that theatre is still surprising and inspiring whilst I find a lot of television formulaic and unsurprising.

**What are the main differences for a writer between a theatre script and any other script?**

The main difference is that there is nowhere to hide. In film you can cut to another scene or in TV it's all close up/midshots but in theatre, you have a live audience who you have to entertain for a couple of hours. The words are everything and the actors and directors rely on a good script to interpret. You have to think of character, dialogue and structure as well as dramatic action and subtext. I think it's difficult to write a good play and people often underestimate how complex a craft it is.

In theatre, I would say that the status of a writer is very high. We get to choose directors (with the theatre that is) and sit in all castings with the director. We also attend rehearsals and generally it is considered very bad form to change a script without the writer's consent.

In radio drama, it's more or less the same but in television and film it's more of a director's medium. They still need a script written, though writers are often not consulted and scripts are changed without consent.

**What are the main obstacles to getting something made and made well?**

It's very difficult at the moment to get plays on. Money is of course the big factor. Or rather, lack of it. It affects everything from theatre's abilities to commission, to the calibre of the director, to the number of actors. A play produced at the National Theatre will have the best sound, set design, actors and lights. A play made in a pub venue will have amazingly dedicated people working there who are good but they will not be able to put on the sorts of plays the National can.

I would also say that 'The Gatekeepers' (as in the artistic directors of theatres) are often from a particular class and race. Their tastes control what goes on their stage and it is often, in my opinion, narrow and eurocentric. Conservative attitudes are a big obstacle in getting something made.

## What do you wish you knew when you were starting out?

It was probably best I didn't know how tough it was going to be! It would definitely have put me off.

## What should be in every show?

A good joke which makes everyone laugh.

## How valuable is an original idea?

They say that all ideas have been done before and Shakespeare did them all. What makes an idea original is one's voice. My idea about a love triangle for example, would be very different from the same idea by another writer. All original ideas are of course valuable!

## How much of a script (when finally made) is yours?

That's a good question. My first reaction would have been to say it's all mine but actually, thinking about it, theatre is collaborative and so whilst the *script* is all mine – the resulting production is a joint venture.

## Pros and cons of: actors.

Pros: Without actors, there would be no plays. They are beautiful people willing to be brave onstage, to speak your words and lift it off the page.

Cons: The truth? They can be a bit needy and self-obsessed.

**Pros and cons of: directors.**

Pros: Without directors breathing life into the words on a page and interpreting them for actors and crew, we writers would be lost. They are incredibly inspiring conductors who know how to make a play work on the stage.

Cons: Oh blimey. They can be a bit bossy and power-mad sometimes. But then that's part of their job!

**Pros and cons of: producers.**

Pros: I have worked with some fantastic producers who are brilliant at putting teams together, galvanising everyone into action and getting a show off the ground.

Cons: Producers often have a lot of financial pressure on them to get a show making money and that can affect relationships with the 'creatives'.

**Pros and cons of: writers.**

Pros: Writers can be funny, inventive, collaborative, brilliant and original.

Cons: We can sometimes be over-protective of our work, defensive and sometimes vulnerable.

**Give me an example of something that can be done on the stage well but less so in other media.**

There are many things, but for me the magic of stage is in speech to a live audience.

Speeches delivered by a character onstage work a lot better than in film. In the theatre, you can enjoy word play and the nuances, power and emotion an actor brings to the piece. 'Playing to the Gods', a bit of circus clowning onstage – all this is the stuff of Shakespeare and works well onstage. In film, it's more about pictures and in TV, if someone suddenly started making a big speech, we would say it was 'too theatrical'.

Think of Obama's speech when he first got the Presidency. Such a historic moment! So many people in the audience listening. Or the opening Olympics ceremony in London. I saw them both on the TV but I know people who were present at both events and they said the effect of being in the audience was magical, grand and made the person feel special and privileged to have been part of the event. That's what theatre gives us which no other medium can.

\* \* \*

Passion, excitement and the need for a good joke – all qualities I've found in my good friend Joss Bennathan. Joss is a theatre director. He describes his job as taking a play 'from page to stage and making it work in three-dimensions, in front of an audience.'

At the time of writing, Joss has nearly finished directing his 49th production and is about to embark on the 50th. His work encompasses a vast and diverse range of plays, from 15th-century tragedy and 16th-century comedy, to the British premieres of new American plays, from the louche world of 19th-century Paris to the repressed world of 1950s genteel poverty. And a musical version of *The A-Team*.

His work has been listed twice in amongst the *Independent*'s 'Best Five Plays In London', his last London production was described in *The Times* as 'majestic' and 'overwhelming', and many of Britain's leading drama schools keep inviting him back to direct their students. He's an experienced script editor and his books for Drama teachers include *Making Theatre: The Frazzled Drama Teacher's Guide To Devising*. He has curated and co-ordinated several festivals of devised theatre.

Joss concludes the CV he wrote for me with these words: 'so all in all, he knows how to deconstruct a script and how to construct one. Which is what you need to know if you want to write plays.'

**DQ: Describe what you do, exactly.**

JB: I direct plays. Sometimes I produce them too. What's the difference? The director is in charge of the creative process while the producer provides the wherewithal, whether that be structure, framework, venue and/or cash, to enable that process. But it is – or should be – a collaborative relationship so a director may well be involved in aspects of the overall production process and vice versa.

Directing involves far more than just assembling a group of actors with the right chemistry and bringing a script from page to stage. A director often needs to be a bizarre combination of nursemaid, firefighter and sergeant major: cajoling, persuading, reassuring, challenging, and demanding as required. It's like spinning plates. You also need an efficient deputy stage manager (that's the one who's in the rehearsal studio) with social skills, as well as an inspired design team. Oh, and effective publicity. No point in all that work if nobody comes to see the production!

## When did you realise you wanted to make a living from writing?

I've written a lot. I've written two source books for Drama teachers and edited a third. I've written numerous education resource packs for various plays and theatre companies. I've written more grant applications than I care to remember, to raise money to fund work. Give me a commission, a fee and a deadline (above all, give me a cast iron reason, 'Your house will be repossessed and your children taken into care' if you fail to meet the deadline) and I'll write for you. But, despite the fact I've earned significant amounts of money writing, I'm not a writer, because I don't burn to write.

Many years ago, I was at university with a woman who is now one of Britain's leading playwrights. I remember, in one of those drunken student union bar conversations, she announced that, if she was in prison and had nothing to write with or on, she'd be scratching words onto the bricks of her cell walls with her fingernails. I was impressed by her passionate conviction. But I remember thinking, 'Nah … that's not me. I wouldn't do that. I'd be planning my escape.' My preferred form of creativity is more convivial. I like being in a roomful of people. Writing is too solitary for me.

**What did you like about theatre?**

I like theatre because it is an ephemeral experience. A performance can't be captured or replicated. If you watch a film twice, it's the same both times. If you go to see a production twice, it will be different each time because it's happening in the here and now. Jean-Louis Barrault (film buffs will know he played the white faced mime Baptiste in *Les Enfants du Paradis*) once said that, 'Theatre is the art of the present moment'. That's why my company is called Present Moment because theatre happens now – wherever and whenever 'now' is. Film doesn't do that. TV doesn't do that. A film or a TV programme is an artefact. Theatre is a communal experience: it needs an audience to complete the circle. Not just their connection with what's onstage but with each other. Those connections and their responses mean that every performance is a unique variation of the production.

If the question is also about making theatre – the process that leads to that ephemeral, communal experience – then I like being part of a team. Well, more honestly, I like leading a team. I'm good at getting a disparate group of people to work with a sense of common purpose, by creating a sense of ensemble where everyone, regardless of the size of part or the backstage task, feels that their contribution is valued and essential to the success of the whole. Arguably, that's the basis of good management in pretty much any situation. The difference is that, when making theatre, you are creating a world. I like that, too. I'm a bit of an evangelist about the need to build bridges between the world of the audience and the world of the play, enabling them to make connections, empathise, understand. If you merely reflect an audience's experience, you run the risk of trapping them in that experience and confirming their prejudices. And why would you want to do that?

**What are the main differences for a writer between a theatre script and any other script?**

The first thing that springs to mind is the obvious one of point of view. In film, TV, even radio, the writer and the director get to decide point of view, to direct attention. Unlike theatre, the audience have no peripheral vision. You can see things in theatre, which you can't in radio; but unlike film or TV you can't be sure the audience pays attention to them – hence the clunky exposition that occurs when the playwright has a crisis of confidence. Of course, it's a director's job to do their best to ensure that an audience's attention is focused in the right part of the stage and action at the right time.

The fact that audience and characters inhabit the same physical space in the theatre and go through time together creates a very different kind of suspension of disbelief from that required in other media.

In radio, you go all out to make it sound real, because the medium is so unreal. In film, TV, ditto – the audience have to believe, however crazy the situation. They have to agree to fill in the blanks (no smell, no depth). They have to collaborate. Theatre is completely different; the audience is faced with living breathing actors, who can be too, distractingly, real. The imaginative leap asked of the theatre audience is a very different one. It's much deeper.

There's something about the different architecture and rhythm of theatre, too. In general, theatre allows us to exist in real time or at least in the same place with the same characters for far longer than we expect to do in film or on TV. This means that you can create a unique form of claustrophobia and intensity in theatre.

Theatre tends to be organized into longer scenes – that's why you can usually tell when a play has been (poorly) adapted into a film. Although contemporary theatre is far more likely to feature short scenes, and a play can move backwards and forwards in time and space, you can't create meaning through juxtaposition in the way that you can in film or TV. In *American Psycho*, for example (the film, not the recent stage musical version), Patrick Bateman asks a character, at a meal in a restaurant, whether he wants another Martini. Then we jump cut to that character, sprawled, drunk in Bateman's apartment. You can't do that in theatre.

**What are the main obstacles to getting something made and made well?**

Cost and interference.

Cost first. It's a difficult medium within which to make money. Income, and therefore any profit – unless or even if you have grants and donations to subsidise you – is determined by the number of people you can fit into a theatre. Even if you have a venture capital or a subsidized theatre, it's a risky investment. No one knows what will sell or why a particular show will capture the public imagination and another won't. Publicity campaigns can't buy audiences, as recent early closures of high profile West End musicals confirm. So, if there is no money available or not much, you need someone who is willing to invest their time and emotion and energy in putting your play on. That's why so much fringe theatre is 'profit-share', a euphemism if ever there was one: there is rarely any profit to share. But actors want to act and writers want their work staged so it's a buyer's market.

Secondly, interference. I'm grateful to say this applies less to a director than it does to a playwright, although it has been known and in any case we're talking about how to write plays rather than how to direct musicals based on Spiderman's exploits! Any budding playwright will have experienced the quasi-subterranean world of rehearsed readings. Everyone chips in with their two pennyworth. In my experience, if the first draft of a play has something, then the second is a backward step because the poor playwright is trying to take on every opinion, no matter how contradictory. Some of these comments and insights will be helpful: most first drafts tell too much and show too little, most feature unnecessary reiteration of theme or moral. However, as a rough rule of thumb, the more people who have – or assume – a right or obligation to provide feedback on work-in-progress (up to and including rehearsals and previews), the less likely it is that the playwright's original vision and inspiration will be realised.

**What should be in every show?**

A reason to keep watching. An audience doesn't need to know from the start who the characters are or why what is happening is happening. But we do need to want to find out what happens next. I often suggest to new writers that they deconstruct and analyse the opening scenes of their ten favourite plays, to find out what makes a good beginning.

## How valuable is an original idea?

Originality is often unsung and unappreciated. Notoriously, Vincent van Gogh didn't sell a single painting in his lifetime. The Velvet Underground and Nick Drake have had huge influence on music but their sales during their lifetimes barely made triple figures. Harold Pinter bestrides 20th century British theatre like a colossus: the reviews of his first plays, such as *The Birthday Party*, were so vicious, confounded and negative that they nearly ended his career.

So, originality is risky. Given the cost of theatre-making, is it any wonder a producer will prefer to transpose a movie (hello *Ghost*, hello *Dirty Dancing*, oh look, here comes *Fatal Attraction*), or construct a musical's storyline out of songs that people know already. Given the cost of West End theatre tickets, many punters will plump for the familiar.

Yet this is not an argument for cynically deciding to write something merely because you think it will sell. Apart from anything else, it won't, necessarily. For every *Mamma Mia!* or *Jersey Boys*, there are at least five *Viva Forever!s* or whatever that Blondie musical was called. Some years ago, I was asked to direct a musical version of *The A-Team*. It sold out every performance at the Gilded Balloon in Edinburgh that year but the reason that the audience loved it was that the writer really, really loved the TV series. He was one of those kids who organized others in the playground – except, for him, it was always episodes of *The A-Team*.

For me what is important has less to do with originality and more to do with finding your own, distinctive voice. That voice may be influenced by those who have gone before. It may be totally unique. But it needs to be from the heart.

## How much of a script (when finally made) is yours?

I can only speak from a director's perspective. Making theatre is collaborative and interpretive. Every time an actor opens their mouth they are interpreting. Every time an actor moves or gestures onstage they are interpreting. Such choices will be guided by a director but all of this assumes that a script is a blueprint.

Playwrights such as Eugene O'Neill or Terence Rattigan provide copious stage directions and character descriptions, specifying tone of voice, whether an actor is standing or sitting and so on. To be fair, sometimes these instructions about what a set looks like and when a character moves are because the acting edition is taken from the prompt copy of the original production. Some playwrights or their literary executors impose rigid restrictions before they will license a production. The estate of Samuel Beckett is notorious for this. Still others – Christopher Durang and Tony Kushner spring to mind – provide lengthy forewords or afterwords, urging a particular style of performance.

Some of this is helpful. Mainly, it feels controlling. If you're that bothered, write for a non-collaborative medium or direct it yourself – although that leads to other problems, as my next answer suggests. Otherwise, let it go, boys. But then, I would say that, wouldn't I? As I said, mine is a director's perspective.

## Pros and cons of: directors.

At the risk of sounding pretentious, the director's job is to interrogate the text. That requires a certain distance from the material. It's hard for a playwright to achieve that distance, to see the wood from the trees. That's why, with few exceptions, writers should not direct their own work.

Obviously, as a director, I'm pro-directors. However, there are directors and directors. The image of a Cecil B. DeMille type, striding around in jodhpurs with a megaphone casts a long shadow.

## Pros and cons of: actors.

On balance, I like actors. Given that I spend most of my working day with them, what kind of masochistic fool would I be if I didn't? I like their capacity to be playful. I like their willingness to take risks. While it's not a hard job in the way that, say, teaching all day every day or working down a mine is a hard job, there are emotional risks involved. An actor has to mine dark, uncomfortable places in their imagination or experience. Then there's the occupational hazard of being judged and found wanting on a regular basis, either when an actor doesn't get a job or when reviews of their performance are unkind. So I like their core of steel too.

Mind you, each of the characteristics lauded in the previous paragraph has its downside. Having access to your emotions can lead to a state of arrested development, self-absorption or neurosis. The constant rejection associated with the job can lead people to need constant reassurance or can corrode them with envy. Even the best is capable of losing perspective and throwing a tantrum or two – but then, so are most people in most jobs in the thick of it all.

There are certain types of actor that it's best to avoid. Passive aggressors. Those who need to galvanise their creativity by creating an enemy (usually the director) or stirring the shit. And of course, there are those whose ego runs away with them after a little or a lot of success: the best actors serve the text, not their ego.

## Pros and cons of: producers.

The ideal producer is like the ideal landlord: they take care of everything as soon as it needs to be taken care of.

The ideal producer is like the dream parent. Supportive but with boundaries. Knowing when to sympathise and when to defend but also when to kick your arse.

The ideal producer does not exist.

## Pros and cons of: writers.

There's a lot to be said for dead playwrights. They don't have to be consulted about pruning their work. Your average five-act revenge tragedy or Restoration comedy features more recaps than your average soap opera, in case members of the original audience had popped out to fight a duel, have sex, or die of the Plague.

When it comes to new work, the playwright may be in the rehearsal studio for some or all of the time. Some are remarkably undefensive of their work, others react to the suggestion that a line or – God help us – a scene be cut with all the fury of a parent told their child should have been left on a hillside at birth. Sometimes, eminence – or a powerful agent – will lead to a playwright throwing their weight around. I speak as a director who discovered once that a producer had agreed to the playwright having casting approval, although mentioning this fact to me had slipped the producer's mind. The writer in question was very keen that their partner be cast in a major role.

The current vogue for immersive theatre and for physical theatre downplays the importance of the writer in favour of the spectacle of the event. Which is a shame: a good blueprint is essential. But, as mentioned elsewhere, it's a collaborative art form. If you don't want your work messed with, go away and write a novel – although bear in mind that some pesky editor may have suggestions...

### Are courses any use?

Depends on the course, really. The great Captain Beefheart – pause for younger readers to look him up – taught his Magic Band to play their instruments. Well, he said he did. At least one of them disputes that. Furiously. Beefheart said that drums cannot be taught, they can only be inferred. So, I think a basic talent or aptitude can be developed via a course, and that an understanding of craft can be gained. But I don't think any course can create talent. What is useful to know in depth? It is useful to know how plays work! I read a lot of work by aspiring playwrights. Some people can plot. Some people can write dialogue. Very few can do both. Most can do neither.

Playwriting is a craft as well as an art. There are many ways that effective drama is structured. Anyone who wants to write plays should read as well as see as many plays as possible, to help understand how to construct a plot.

### Give me an example of something that can be done on the stage well but less so in other media.

Theatre is a form that can explore, express and communicate anything. Two periods of time can exist simultaneously. Time can be slowed down – what else is a slow motion sequence? – or accelerated. *The Royal Hunt of the Sun* famously contains the stage direction, 'They cross the Andes'. I once directed a script that required us to stage the moment of a boiler room explosion extended over a period of ten minutes, inter-cut with the big bang theory. Anything can be represented, but it cannot be represented literally, in the way that an action sequence packed with computer generated special effects in a film does.

In an earlier answer, I wrote about the audience completing the circle. Interestingly, while theatre gets increasingly high-tech, shows that make the audience complicit by drawing attention to non-literal representation continue to appeal. *The Woman in Black* has been running in the West End for a quarter century. Two actors, a bare stage and a handful of props transform into all manner of people, locations and objects. The play draws attention to the theatrical form. It makes the audience complicit by making a game of the constant transformation. So did the very successful *Stones in His Pockets*. So does the *Jeeves and Wooster* play *Perfect Nonsense*.

All three of those are plays that break the fourth wall, which is to say, characters acknowledge the audience and address them directly. Although, as mentioned earlier, naturalistic plays can feature long scenes and create claustrophobia, so naturalism can be done onstage, but it requires a suspension of disbelief (and a different form of complicity) to TV or film which can be far more naturalistic.

**I know nothing about theatre-writing. How would you explain it to someone who's as ignorant as me?**

I think you will find the following observations, written nearly one hundred years apart, helpful: The American theatre critic, William Archer, in his 1912 book, *Playmaking*, suggested that drama might be called the art of crisis while fiction was the art of gradual development.

This year, in his book *How Plays Work*, the playwright (and playwriting professor) David Edgar pointed out that a play can only present characters via what they say and do – unlike novelists who can write from a character's point of view.

**And finally an exercise. Imagine you're writing a letter to a niece or nephew who wants to write plays for money. Conveying as much information, anecdote, optimism, realism, affection, memory and examples from your own experience as possible, write that letter. And write it long as though you're stuck in a seaside boarding house all week and it's raining and you have time to expand.**

You shouldn't write plays because you want to make money. The brutal truth is that there's not a lot of money in theatre for anyone, and that includes writers. True, it can be a springboard for making money. I first encountered the work of Chris Chibnall (*Broadchurch*, *Doctor Who*) and Toby Whithouse (*Being Human*) via plays they wrote for Soho Theatre. For some, subsidised theatre has certainly provided a training ground for more lucrative writing opportunities.

So, if you want a guaranteed income, do something else. You should write plays because you have something you want to say and you think a play is the best medium within which to say it.

I do a lot of work with drama teachers and GCSE drama students on devising theatre. The questions I ask them are:

- What's the story you want to tell?

- How do you want to tell it?

- Why do you want to tell it?

- What effect do you want to have on the audience?

- How will you create that effect?

I think these are vital questions to ask yourself at some point. I say 'at some point' because you may be one of those writers who needs to write it to find out what you're writing about. Also, it is true that sometimes the writer is not the best person to interpret or explain their own work. As D.H. Lawrence once wrote, 'Never trust the artist, trust the tale.' But you do need to consider what you know about your chosen subject and what insight do you have to offer? That's why so many people write about what they know. I don't think you have to do that, necessarily. I think imagination and empathy can take you to all sorts of places and experiences. But, if you want to write about the plight of trafficked women or farming in Patagonia, then make sure you do your research.

If you must write (and I do mean 'must') a few principles:

- Show, don't tell.

- It is always more interesting (in life as well as theatre) seeing someone trying not to cry than it is seeing someone cry. Similarly, it is always more interesting seeing someone trying not to shout. There are practical as well as artistic reasons for this. An audience needs to be able to understand what is being said. In any case, you don't want the audience sitting there going 'Oh, stop shouting' or 'Stop crying'.

- Avoid excessive stage directions. I understand that you want to suggest how a line might be said. But it's a collaborative process and a creative partnership. Actors are not puppets to be told when to move or how to say a line. They may come up with different, better possibilities than you have!

- It's not the story you tell it's the way that you tell it.

- Avoid hectoring the audience. It raises the hackles. Besides, it's probably occurred to most of your audience that war, poverty and child abuse are not good things.

So, then. Write, if you can't imagine anything else making you happy. And good luck!

## Chapter Nine
# Journalism

Along with prostitution and the law, journalism is the oldest profession and, like prostitutes and lawyers, journalists have always had a bad reputation. If we're not alcoholic cynics doorstepping widows, we're fag-smoking vultures listening to celebrities' voicemails. We fill the evil tabloids with gossip and the broadsheets with columns about how the tabloids are full of gossip. We pervert the English language with our idiotic slang and we killed Princess Diana.

Is it any wonder no self-respecting person ever buys a newspaper or a magazine? No, wait, hang on, newspapers sell millions of copies every day. The more prurient or extreme the paper, the more it sells. Magazines devoted to the lives of celebs clog up the news stands, yet are gone in seconds. It's like these awful things are somehow popular. Mind you, I bet if all the newspapers and magazines were replaced by improving tracts and – you know what? – a newspaper that ONLY PRINTED THE GOOD NEWS, those nice things would be just as popular.

Do stop reading now if you like but the fact is, newspapers and magazines sell because we buy them. And I do mean 'we': it's no good telling me you only read the *Guardian* or the *Telegraph* or the *Dull Thing* so it's not your fault because a) you're lying and b) if you're telling the truth and you're under sixty, what an awful person you must be, with your look-at-me-I'm-above-all-this persona and your tweed pipe and your Greek quotes. I'm assuming.

If you don't read all the papers and all the magazines, you despise popular culture, which means you despise people, which means you're at best one of those divots who lives in a 1930s house and has all Bakelite furniture and at worst a serial culture snob. You certainly shouldn't be reading a book about writing because why? Are you hoping to get some tips on meeting Doctor Johnson in a coffee house? Have you a pamphlet on the Corn Laws you're looking to circulate?

So journalism in all its forms – from stamp collecting mags and rock heritage titles to lurid made-up, mentally ill supermarket tabloids and the *Daily Mail* – exists because it's popular. It sells because people want to read it. The reasons there isn't, as vicars and newsreaders sometimes suggest, a newspaper devoted to Only Good News is because human nature enjoys bad news. We love it when a celebrity gets fat, or when a marriage fails, or the economy collapses, or there's a war. And you know the saying: no news is good news? It's more accurate in reverse: good news is no news. If you don't like news, read one of those weird free newspapers that look like a cult wrote them. Or watch a TV gossip show, where a teenage model who was dropped on his head as a baby tries to read stories out loud about other teenage models who were dropped on their head as a baby.

I'll be dull now and say there are limits. I've met journalists who've broken into people's houses to get material for a story, and I don't care much for phone-hacking and so forth. On the other hand if a prostitute fellates a movie star or a government minister is shown to be corrupt I want to know about it, and that's not going to happen in an over-regulated press, or even one where any sane moral laws operate. Every day journalists make moral choices and sometimes they fail, quite often for mercenary reasons. These people should be hanged. Everyone else is just trying to get along.

Journalism is the single most despised yet essential profession in the world. And I'm not just talking about the investigative journalists who were so important until computer experts discovered they could just upload bulk undigested top-secret information to the net (thereby endangering thousands of lives because, unlike journalists, crusading geeks have no filter, just a burning sense of justice. Which generally ends in someone else being burned. Often literally).

Journalists don't just provide information, they channel it. They mould the information and comment on it. This is apparently a bad thing and I would be against it if I knew anything about science or finance, or if I was a Whitehall insider, or had spent my life building up contacts, experience and knowledge in a specialized but crucial area of modern life. Journalists look at the constant mad flow of news and interpret it, often in a politically biased way; but the best to explain what is happening as it's happening.

I don't just mean news-gatherers. In a culture where we get our news online, on the radio and off the TV, the up-to-date info aspect of newspapers is severely constrained. Not just newspapers: when I worked for the weekly music press, we sold thousands not because of the limpid wit and rapier beauty of the reviews, but because there was no other way to find out what records were coming out, when they were coming out, when bands were touring, and what Bananarama had had for tea that week. In the 21st century, people can find all that out the instant it happens, which is why papers like the *NME* exist online and, more oddly, why so much of the music press sells the past instead of the future.

Newspapers and magazines mediate the news. Which is a way of saying that anyone can understand that they take the unfiltered mulch of everything and pick out the best, or the most important bits. The latest appalling thing said by a footballer, the new breasts of a singer, the class-hate-filled policies of a minister; these are the weathercocks of our culture, and even if we are superbrains who could assimilate this ourselves, we find it easier to pay someone else to do it.

And we pay them according to our prejudices. If we think the world should be nicer, but we want to keep all our stuff, we buy the *Guardian* and its ghost, the *Independent*. If we like being scared by stories about immigrants, we buy the *Mail* and its homunculus, the *Express*. If we are working class or would like to be, we buy the *Mirror* or *The Sun*, and their freakish parody, the *Daily Star*. And so on.

In every way, we get the newspapers we deserve. And the magazines. And the gossip sites. And the blogs. Except for the purposes of this book blogs aren't journalism because if you're not being paid to write, it doesn't count.

(This is an important point, by the way, and one I will come the hell back to later on. There's a massive move, particularly in journalism, and particularly online, towards not paying people. Americans call this 'internship'. Writers call this 'exploitation.' You work, you get paid. That's the basis of all labour transactions. If you don't get paid, it's not work. It's doing someone a favour, or being a victim, or an idiot. The writer, author, broadcaster and former member of Irony Maiden, my friend Stuart Maconie, once met a man who said to him, 'I'm like you, I'm a freelance. I write for free!' Being a freelance doesn't mean you write for free. Get paid. Join a union. Join the NUJ. You have rights, which are being removed, and those removals mean loss of income, loss of copyright and loss of career. Join the NUJ. (There will be more about this sort of thing later. [But really, if you're writing for free you're not a journalist, you're enjoying a hobby. (And now let's get out of these brackets.)])

As you may have guessed, I am a big fan of journalism. I've written newspaper columns, I've done pieces for Sunday magazines, and I've interviewed over a thousand people and reviewed about ten times that many records. They beat the hell out of uninformed blogs, outraged posts on Facebook and Twitter, unfunny satire websites, natural disasters filmed on people's phones, and everything that optimistic bozos say will replace journalism. Yes, it's going through change at the moment but, as you'll know from your study of world history, so is everything else, all the time, forever.

Journalism is great. And maybe that's why you want to be a journalist. Lots of brilliant people have been journalists. (Wiki them, that was a shot in the dark. But they have.) There is no greater writing practise than journalism because you write every day. You have to. Even Charles Dickens had a month to put together a chapter of one of his serialized novels; mind you, if he'd been chucking out ten pages of *Little Dorrit* every day in the *Mirror*, then we'd have seen something. Attack ships off the Shoulder of Mutton, perhaps.

What should you do to become a journalist? Apart, obviously, from contacting your local NUJ representative? When I started, back in the days before anything, I wrote to thirty local newspapers. I think my lack of enthusiasm for being a local newspaperman must have showed as I didn't get many, or maybe any, responses. Later I actually got work by writing an aggressive letter to the editor of the *NME*, Neil Spencer, criticizing his entire magazine. The letter contained the phrase BOB SEGER IS NOT ENOUGH, so you can see that I was easily exercised in those days. Neil invited me to write a review, I reviewed an album I already had (ABC's *Lexicon of Love*) and that was it.

The details have changed a lot in thirty years but the principle is the same (and in fact it's the same for any writing you want to do. In second fact it's the only principle you really need to know about writing at all). Here it is, in its own paragraph:

> Work out what you want to write and where is the best place to write it. When you've done that, find out who are the people who work at that place who choose the writers, and get in touch with them.

There really isn't anything else you need to know. You can get better at writing by writing. You can learn about writing by reading or watching or listening. But if you want people to use your writing, you need to place it, or at least to put it where it can be seen. If you want to write about finance, there's no point contacting the *Guardian Guide*. If you love reviewing television shows, don't approach *The Times Court Circular*. If you feel strongly that immigration should be free and unlimited, don't ask the *Daily Mail* for a column. And so on. Identify your interests, target your editor (or your producer, or your heroine) and proceed accordingly.

Don't be too proud. I am full of admiration for self-confident young men and women, fresh out of private education or Oxbridge who sweep aside their own lack of experience and perform brilliantly at job interviews. Actually I'm not at all; I feel that we are unlikely to experience a shortage of vague, floppy-haired people who are unable to express enthusiasm and perhaps someone else could have a go. Very likely if you are normal, and reading this book, you will not be brimming at the gills with self-belief and the certainty that everything you do is amazing. You will almost certainly be made of doubt and unable to answer questions in a job interview without spilling your beta blockers.

I once spoiled a perfectly good teenage achievement awards ceremony by giving a speech whose gist was this: don't follow your dream. The purpose of the awards, quite sensibly, was to encourage young people to follow their dream. My argument was that following your dream is great if a) you succeed entirely at following your dream b) you have a dream in the first place and c) despite being only seventeen or whatever, you are quite happy to travel down the track towards your dream and will never change your mind.

When I was seventeen I wanted to be an actor. I was writing poems and articles and even an attempted novel at the same time but for some reason I was convinced that acting was the thing for me. I was, and am, a terrible actor, but I wanted to act. If I'd followed my dream, I'd now be a bad, unhappy actor. Instead I did law at college, a subject I had no aptitude for, and when I left college, with a bad degree and no interest in law, I wrote to the *NME*. Even then I did not know that I wanted to write; I hadn't even suppressed this ambition, it hadn't occurred to me that this was a possibility.

Be adaptable. Secure a platform for experiment. Student loans don't make college a great place for messing about these days, but try and find a writing environment with flexibility. Maybe you're lucky and you know you're a playwright or a novelist or a sports reporter; most probably if you're just starting out, you're someone who knows they want to write but not much else.

Some novelists start out as poets. Some poets start out as novelists. Many writers begin as journalists. Cameron Crowe, the film-maker, famously began as a writer for *Rolling Stone* magazine. You may well be doing a thing that later you won't want to do. (Maybe you're a multi-platform writer; increasingly people find themselves writing books, scripts, comics, and everything else.)

When I wrote for the *NME*, it was less the fanziney rock reporter paper it is now, and more closely resembled a website like *The Huffington Post* or *The Onion AV Club*. Most of the writers stuck to reviewing records and gigs and interviewing bands, but some of us were given the freedom to experiment. You could write short comedy pieces, so long as they had some connection to music. You could, if you were me, write the entire gossip page in the style of Flann O'Brien's *The Brother* (I did that) or the spoken introduction to Dexy's Midnight Runners' 'This is What She's Like'. If you were Stuart Maconie and Andrew Collins, you could invent a *Believe It Or Not* column whose most famous lie – that the TV presenter Bob Holness played saxophone on Gerry Rafferty's 'Baker Street' – is still repeated. You might even, if you were lucky enough to be Steven Wells or me, be given a page each week to fill purely with scabrous and vile comedy and insult.

This isn't pure vanity and nostalgia; I am about to make a point. Steven and I wrote a column called *Culture Vulture* (aka Ride The Lizard, because Swells was a genius) and this was read by the radio producer Armando Iannucci who offered us work on his new radio show *On The Hour*.

Everything leads to everything else, if you let it. The *NME* isn't a hothouse for radio presenters and comedy writers these days, but the web is full of places which require content. Go there, create a portfolio of work (oh, and get paid for it) and write about as many different things as you can. Write in different styles, interview people who you didn't know were interesting (all interviews should be interesting because there really are no dull people. If your interview is dull, that's your fault, not the head of marketing at Grey Pots Inc).

Journalism is a great place to write because sometimes you're forced to think in a restrictive and unfamiliar house style (obstacles lead to inspiration) and sometimes you have the space to try something different. I wrote for the *Observer* in the 1980s and, being unable to report from war zones or cover fashion, I looked for areas that had not been done. I wasn't, admittedly, great at this, but I did get a piece about the portable map books of London commissioned, the A to Z and its rival, the Streetfinder. And this is how I met the great Phyllis Pearsall, one of the most extraordinary women of the 20th century (look her up), and how I found out what mapmakers do to deter copyists (they insert a fake address into their maps). Experience, surprise, knowledge.

When you have identified the place where you want to begin working – which should not necessarily be the place you want to end up working – it's time to make approaches. And now the Catch-22 effect comes into play. You can't entice an editor if you have nothing to show her; but if you haven't published anything, there's nothing to show anyone. These days life is a bit easier because you can self-publish, but if you do send someone a piece you did for a blog or similar, I'd make sure it was the best thing you can do. By which I mean nobody cares what you think of something you saw on television or what you heard on the radio. If you want to be a journalist, you should try and provide something that somebody might actually want. Interviews with a person of interest are good. A review of something that isn't widely available. The last confession of a mass murderer. Anything that might have currency, in at least three senses of the word.

Of course, you may not be able to provide any of that, but don't worry. If you're a good writer, you can write a spec piece on something else, at least to show how well you can write. Incorporate more than one skill. If you have an opinion, make it at least different and at best backed up with research, with quotes and with first-hand information. And keep it up. Send another piece, a different one. And another. And keep it up.

There is an art to submitting. How do you write that email or make that phone call? If someone asks you to send them stuff, do you bombard them or do you send that one perfect article? And most importantly of all – how long do you wait to chase up a reply? (Because nobody ever writes back the same day and says, 'Amazing stuff! Come in and choose your salary!') These people are busy. If they weren't, they wouldn't be worth writing to. And busy means they have things to be getting on with. You are not at the forefront of their mind. Remember this: just because all you can think about is the piece you submitted and did they get it and are they reading it and have they forgotten and so on does not mean that they've even had a chance to open your reply email.

That said, there are some right chancers out there. Most people will get back to you, when they have time. Most people will write a considered response to you, when they have a moment. And most people would rather find a great new writer than not. But some people need a push (some people need a kicking, but later for that). I would say use a sliding scale for reminders – give the person you wrote to a month to reply, then send them a polite email asking if they've had a chance to look at your piece. Don't be arrogant; just be honest and normal. Then if they say they're going to look at it or not, wait another two weeks if you've heard nothing, and then ask again (and don't be pissy and say, 'this is my second attempt to get a reply from you'; for all you know, their family have been kidnapped). And then a week. And then just blow up their cars. Because some people deserve it. There is the apocryphal perhaps story of the two sitcom writers who sent a script to a TV comedy producer (TV comedy producers are the worst) and waited a year before sending their script a first birthday card, care of said producer.

Be polite, be persistent, and be aware that you might be a genius, but right now you are a genius wrapped up in an enigma contained in a person nobody cares about.

And you will notice, again, that I have not included here a list of magazines and periodicals with the personal telephone numbers and email addresses of prominent editors and writers. This is partly because I do not wish to annoy the ones I know; and also because, as I will say here from time to time, if you can't work out who to contact at a newspaper, you're not going to be much of a journalist. Unless, as often happens, it's your dad's newspaper.

I'll end this section with a few practical tips:

**Interviews.** Horrible hard work, but do your research into your subject. Write down a list of questions but be prepared to make up questions as you go. Go with the flow of the interview even if that means following the interviewee somewhere new. I once witnessed a radio interview where the show's presenter had been told the musician he was talking to was a country singer. Every question was about country music, the importance of country in the singer's work, her favourite country songs, and so on. Her first reply was, 'I don't know, I'm not a country singer.' Her second reply was, 'Like I said, I'm not a country singer.' And so on. Be flexible (but also interrupt if they lose their own thread). Transcribe the interview as soon as you can, as it's less painful to get it out of the way (transcribing is the worst thing about writing, it takes hours and your voice and questions sound awful). Write down any atmosphere you can recall. And don't be afraid to ditch most of their answers; it's an article, not an interrogation transcript.

Oh, and don't worry about saying 'she said' or 'he said' a lot. It always drives me mad to see a quote followed by the words, 'she grinned' or 'he chuckled.' Try grinning a sentence and you'll see what I mean, he growled.

**Reviews.** Up to you, but give the odd example here and there to centre it for the reader – actors' names, song titles, memorable scenes and so on. And if you can, don't complain that you thought the thing you're reviewing would be X and then criticize it for not being X. 'I thought this novel would be a searing satire but in fact it was a love story.' Write your own searing satire if that's what you desire.

**Columns.** Completely up to you, but an on-the-surface logical argument always helps. As does a completely insane point of view. Readers love to be outraged; they don't always read you to be assured the world is fine. Sometimes they read you to hate you. And columns are really the only time the 'I' word is not only acceptable, it's compulsory. You're not a badly translated French robot; never say 'one.'

**Making things up.** Definitely up to you (and the lawyers). As a music journalist, I made a lot of things up, but I developed a rule – I'd always be nice to people if I forgot to go to the show or didn't play the album. If you are going to make a review up, make it look convincing. Play a few songs from the album. Fast forward the DVD. Read someone else's review. But it's probably best these days not to make it up. (Good mental exercise if you do, though.)

**Editing the letters page.** The letters and emails you get will generally be boring, or insane. Make it up.

**Finally: join a union.** Join the NUJ. Join the Writer's Guild of Great Britain. You're in a profession which the general public associates with dishonesty, sleaze and getting rich quick. Most of your colleagues are honest, fairly moral and not well-off. Management will steal your copyrights (try and retain ownership of your work; when photographers do, it can pay for their retirement). Governments will try and restrict your freedom. So join a union.

And remember; journalism, more than any other profession (well, nearly), puts you near other, interesting people. Use it to make contacts. You may not befriend the people you write about, but you can be of mutual use to one another (this is partly why I enjoyed interviewing comedians; they're always looking for writers who understand what they're trying to do).

Journalism. There's a reason it's the oldest profession in the world. It's great.

## Chapter Ten
# Poetry

I used to write poetry, as a child and as a teenager. Then I got embarrassed, and then I thought I couldn't do it, and then I knew I couldn't do it, so I stopped. Every so often, now that I am steeped in age, I try writing poems again, and sometimes I like the result, but I'm very conscious that I haven't put the hours in; that is, I haven't read enough poetry or written enough to be good. But I keep trying, as you will see.

This chapter's guest host is a real poet, however. He's called Dan O'Brien and his debut poetry collection *War Reporter* was published in 2013 by CB Editions in London and Hanging Loose Press in Brooklyn. *War Reporter* received the UK's Fenton Aldeburgh First Collection Prize, and was shortlisted for the Forward Prize for Best First Collection. O'Brien's play *The Body of an American* had its European premiere in an extended run at the Gate Theatre in London and Royal & Derngate Theatre in Northampton in 2014. *The Body of an American* is published by Oberon Books. Originally from New York, O'Brien lives in Los Angeles with his wife, actress Jessica St. Clair, and their daughter Isobel.

Dan was kind enough to engage in the following conversation via email.

**DQ: Poems used to be rhyming couplets, intricate language and full of classical reference. Do they still have to be?**

DO'B: Maybe not so much the rhyming couplets. While there are certainly a lot of poets writing in formal verse today, in general the last hundred years has opened up ideas about what a poem should and shouldn't be.

'Intricate language' in poetry? – most definitely. Of course, intricacy is relative. But poetry is written by and for people who want to communicate the complexity of life via the complexity of language.

As for classical references in poems, yes there's probably less of that going around these days. Still, contemporary poems will allude to other poems, stories, plays, films, myths, both classical and cultural. It's probably impossible not to do so. In lesser poems this kind of thing can seem pretentious, like a borrowing of importance. In the best poems any sort of allusion or reference feels like a natural facet of the voice, the story, the language and music of the poem – just another way of communicating.

**Is a poem nowadays bad if it's old fashioned?**

That depends on what you mean by 'old-fashioned.' There are fantastic poems written today that follow strict patterns of form, meter, and rhyme that will probably strike many as old-fashioned in a dry-as-dust way. But many others will admire the formalist poet's skill, and feel moved by this continuation of tradition.

If by old-fashioned you mean outmoded cultural ideas, like poems that praise the glory of war or lament the folly of woman, then yes, that kind of stuff's pretty lame.

### What's the difference between a bad poem and a good one?

Poems I consider good move me with an economy, precision, and complexity of language. Poems I dislike are boring, obvious, sloppy, redundant, reductive, tin-eared…

### When you're reading a poem what do you hope to get from it?

I hope to feel like I know the poet. And for that to happen the poet needs to be honest with me as she writes about something important that she doesn't understand, as she uses the writing of the poem itself as an attempt to gain that understanding. I think life is basically lonely, and I read poems in the hope of feeling less that way.

### When you're writing a poem, what do you intend it to be?

I intend my poems to be honest, moving, intimate, precise, musical, surprising, and about something I can't really put into words. Mostly I want to connect with my reader, to make him feel what I'm feeling, or to make him feel something in response. I want the poem to be beautiful too, of course, or to feel beautiful, to myself and to readers, though I don't know how to define beauty, and I hope I don't ever have to.

## What do all good poems contain?

There's obviously a heightened attention to language in a good poem – attending to the meaning and subtle connotations of each word, to the sound of each word, to the sense and sound of the words together, to what line breaks and stanza breaks communicate to a reader. For those interested in form, a good poem demonstrates the poet's ability to explore the content of his poem within the received structure – and stricture – of a sonnet, say, or a sestina.

Good poems deal in metaphor, simile, figurative language – all in an attempt to communicate thoughts and emotions that feel somehow beyond the reach of everyday, literal language.

But fundamentally, and at the risk of repeating myself, 'good' poems look honestly at what the poet finds difficult, challenging, overwhelming (even overwhelmingly joyful) about life.

## What is the broadest definition of a poem for you?

Song without music, or with only the music of the spoken voice.

**Can you name for us three poems which 'do it' for you, and explain how and why without expensive quotes?**

Here are three poems that have done it for me lately.

### *'My Mother' by Patrick McGuinness*

> How I think about her now is how
> a thought is said to cross the mind:
> like a bird's shadow as it flies,
> dragging its span in darkness along the ground.

This is the entire poem. I admire the elegance of the language, how precisely it captures in metaphor the complexity of the most fundamental relationship. This poem isn't confessional, I don't learn anything factual about McGuinness's life, but I feel that he's trying to communicate to me a complicated experience of love and loss – probably resentment and anger too, though maybe I'm projecting here (and a good poem allows you to project).

Notice also the gentle vowel rhymes of 'how' and 'ground,' of 'mind' and 'flies.' This is rhyme I can live with: subtle, almost conversational, never artificial. Rhyme and rhythm here simply add to the beauty of the poem, which tells me implicitly that the poet has great love for his mother.

## 'The Visit' by Jane Kenyon

The talkative guest has gone,
and we sit in the yard
saying nothing. The slender moon
comes over the peak of the barn.

The air is damp, and dense
with the scent of honeysuckle....
The last clever story has been told
and answered with laughter.

With my sleeping self I met
my obligations, but now I am aware
of the silence, and your affection,
and the delicate sadness of dusk.

Jane Kenyon's poems are astonishingly accurate. She captured external – and internal, that is, emotional – settings powerfully. Here again I enjoy, as with McGuinness, an easy musicality, full of subtle rhymes and rhythms. Deceptively casual, her poems have a miniaturist's talent for detail.

Kenyon's poems are mysterious. And not like in lesser poems where dense language can seem like a kind of intellectual code to be deciphered; rather what is mysterious here is what is mysterious about living. The speaker, after an evening of fun with friends, falls into herself and her loved one with relief, with sadness, perhaps sadness simply at the awareness of loss and mortality, perhaps as she senses an encroaching depression (a condition from which Kenyon suffered). As in the best poems 'The Visit' evokes and instils these thoughts and feelings, without ever explaining them.

### 'Adolescence' by Larry Levis

You get the feeling that Levis jotted his poems down in a notepad, without any painstaking revision. This is an illusion, probably, as his poems, while longer and more discursive than most, tell us only what we need to know, and with great urgency and power.

'Adolescence' opens with a description of a cemetery:

> ...huge trees, rooted in such quiet,
> Arch over the tombstones as if in exultation,
> As if they inhaled starlight.
> Their limbs reach
> Toward each other & their roots must touch the dead.

This is about as 'poetic' as Levis gets, typically. Immediately he's back to simply telling us:

> When I was fifteen,
> There was a girl who loved me; whom I did not love, & she
> Died, that year, of spinal meningitis.

Levis's description of the subsequent death of the girl's father is likewise straightforward, yet shocking again in its honesty, its precise and vivid language:

> Her father died, a year later, in a Sierra lumber camp.
> He had been drinking steadily all week,
> And was dealing cards
> When the muscle of his own heart
> Kicked him back into his chair so hard its wood snapped.

The rest of this poem is an elaboration on the poet's first experience of death, and his struggle to come to terms with death once more in middle age. In some ways, of course, adolescence is a death of innocence, of childhood, yet here Levis personifies Death itself as an adolescent, recklessly taking others' lives. This is a darkly majestic and deeply sad poem.

## Do you have to be a full-time poet to be any good or can anyone write a decent poem?

Even famous poets need a day job. Wallace Stevens was an insurance executive, famously. Unless you're independently wealthy you won't be able to write poetry nine to five, and I'm not sure you'd want to: it's dangerous to chain your muse to a treadmill.

## Can you make a living as a poet?

Most journals that publish your poem will pay you with a copy or two of the issue. Poetry collections pay little in royalties because, sadly, so few people read them. Poetry contests always require an entrance fee. So no: no living.

That said, many poets enjoy the freedom of *not* having to make a living off their art. (Perhaps 'enjoy' is too strong a word.) And, at least in the US, it seems like most poets teach writing and/or literature somewhere, which seems to keep the lights on.

**What are your views on:**

1) Comic verse: I haven't read much that I've actually found comical, though good poems of all stripes have humorous or ironic elements. Life is funny, obviously, sometimes so funny it makes you cry. But something that bills itself as 'comic verse' seems like a throwback to another era, at least to me, an era I don't care about.

2) Greetings-card verse: Terrible. Though I don't make a habit of reading it. Why not buy a blank card and write your own sappy words? (Though maybe it's not a bad day-job for a poet? I'll have to look into that.)

3) Doggerel: Not sure what it is exactly. If it's dogshit poetry then I'm against it.

**What makes a poem nowadays different to a poem two hundred years ago?**

A lot of contemporary poetry is less formal. If anything – and I can't prove this – I suspect that while fewer people read poetry, there's a wider spectrum of style and content out there today. No matter how you write your poems there's a decent chance you'll find some readers somewhere.

I also suspect that two hundred years ago poetry was more of a public performance, and less obviously personal than a lot of poetry today. Like Western culture in general we've become more confiding, even exhibitionistic in our poetry, for better and for worse.

**What should never be in a poem?**

I don't think anything shouldn't be in a poem. The 20th century is supposed to have taught us that. William Carlos Williams's 'This Is Just To Say' (1934) is a celebrated poem about plums that reads like a note taped to the refrigerator door.

Maybe racism, sexism, homophobia, etc., should be left out of poems? Though good poems are often 'about' these things, too.

**And finally, I have made the supreme sacrifice. I wrote a draft of a poem which I never completed. I like the idea (which I stole from *The Children's Bo*ok by A.S. Byatt) and I'd like to improve or complete or maybe forget about the poem, depending on how it goes. If you're up for it, could you review it for me, with bluntly honest suggestions and raw opinion? Not for my benefit, but so we can see how a poet looks at a poem, technically, subjectively and any other ways.**

## Here is the poem.

I sat in the nest, full and ready.

I had bested my brothers and sisters and their food was mine.

Now it was time to go, and I went.

My parents bereft, I shouldn't wonder; we don't look back.


And as I rose up I saw others coming with me

From other nests and other trees

Drawn to the invisible arrow.

Others, who looked the same, a new family in the sky.

And I was them and they were me.


We were the same, who'd never known we were different

But now, returning from African clamour

We'd rather be with warblers, wagtails, pipits,

Anyone who isn't us.

I like this poem. You've undersold your poetic chops, I think. I don't teach poetry, and I'm not a scholar or critic, so I fear I'm going to be giving you some fairly subjective suggestions. But you asked for it:

First off – choose a title! Even if it's just a working title. A title is like the frame through which your reader will view your poem. Or maybe it's like the first line of your poem. Whatever it is, I know a title is important, and helpful when writing.

There's a simplicity of metaphor here – young people as young birds – which is clear and somewhat moving. That said, it's a bit simplistic, thematically speaking. Nothing wrong with simplicity of expression, but simplicity of theme can let your more mature readers down.

Now, you say it's not finished, so maybe the nuance I'm looking for will come from how you revise and develop this metaphor. Can you communicate more complexity, more irony, so that the climax of the poem is some kind of epiphany or realization or startling question about adolescence?

In general when you revise I'd encourage you to search for more specific, surprising, revealing language. For example in your first line the speaker says he was 'full and ready,' two somewhat bland words. What would be implied if the speaker says rather that he was 'fat and anxious' or 'stuffed and itching' (as in 'itching' to fly the nest). These are probably not good suggestions, in the particular, but I hope you get my gist. I like your more figurative language, like the 'invisible arrow' all young people follow towards maturity – this is very evocative, and communicates poetically rather than prosaically. I'd encourage you to search for more figurative language throughout this poem.

Your final stanza is promising – I like 'African clamour,' and I'm always a sucker for the specific naming of birds. But I'm not sure I understand what you're after here ultimately. It's not important to me that I understand a poem intellectually, only that I 'get it' emotionally. The speaker in this stanza seems changed – from revelling in liberation and a sense of sameness with his peers, to desiring separation from them. But I'm not sure when or why or how this change occurred. Developing this inchoate aspect of your poem will go a long way in complicating (in a good way) the simplicity I noted above.

Thanks for putting up with my thoughts about your poem, David, and about poems in general. I continue to write poetry in large part because I *don't* know what I'm doing, and God help me if I ever do.

**Not at all. That was only mildly painful and I felt better afterwards, which is always good. I shall ingest and revise.**

\* \* \*

Not much to add there, except a small and odd but relevant detail. The poem I wrote does have a title, but I forgot to add it to the document when I sent it. It's called 'Cuckoo'; students of interpretation may care to reread the poem and see how Dan's notes on the importance of titles apply to it.

I'd just add to Dan's brilliant comments my own belief that a poem is like a novel, a kite or anything; just because you can't make hundreds of them doesn't mean you won't be able to make one good one (although the more you make, the better they will probably be).

# Afterword

I think that's everything.

Of course it isn't. There are lots of areas I haven't covered – computer games, for one, and non-fiction books for another. But this will do for now. I really only wanted to mention two more things.

The first is nice and practical; it's the whole business of getting paid. Freelance groups all over the net will tell you how hard it is to persuade clients to pay you for the work you've done, and indeed will frequently assume you're doing this for love (of what, they never say. Them, perhaps).

Getting paid is everything, and it's hard work. So here is my very short guide to getting paid.

1. Listen to the Accounts Department. Generally, you will be paid by an accounts department, who may or may not issue invoices or make you fill out tiresome forms every month. Most of the people who work in accounts are friendly, helpful and, if you don't treat them as inferiors, on your side. So as soon as you've established your position as

Someone Who's Done Some Work, find out
how the system works. Do you invoice? If so,
who do you invoice? What form of words is
your invoice? These things matter.

2. Find out the Chain of Payment. If you've
   invoiced and not been paid, it doesn't
   necessarily mean you've been hired by
   crooks. It could just be their payments
   system is awfully slow. Or it could be that
   one of the people who signs off on your
   account, or authorizes your electronic
   payment or even, occasionally, signs your
   cheque, is on holiday, or lazy. If your
   money is late, politely ask your new friend
   in accounts what might be causing the
   delay. Ask if there's anything you can do.
   Or anyone you can speak to. Think of your
   money inching its way towards you and
   getting stuck on little boulders as it does so.
   Remove the boulders.

3. Be nice. Why would someone stuck in an
   office want to help someone with a carefree
   freelance life who has no manners?

4. If you still don't get paid, ask around. Do
   other writers have problems with this client?
   Find out what they do.

5. Join a union. If you are waiting for money from crooks, or dodgy clients, or just some scumbag who's sold your copyrights without asking you, a union can help. They have experience, and they have lawyers. What else could anyone ask for?

And always remember; it's your money. You don't owe them. They owe you.

So there's that. The other thing I wanted to mention was that Dan Brown quote at the very start of the book, the one about enjoying having written. Lots and lots of writing is no fun. Arguably, the best writing is often no fun. If you're enjoying yourself, you might not be writing something other people will enjoy. And even if you are, the sheer volume and effort of writing something long or something complex is often just painful. Which is why Dan Brown enjoys having written; it's great to know you've done it, you've filled the pages, you've created the bon mots, you've told the story. Now you can enjoy someone else enjoying your work.

If you've read this far, thank you very much. But now it's time to quit stalling and get out there and do some writing.

And there it is. My final piece of advice. Write!

# Bibliography

- Christopher Booker: *The Seven Basic Plots*. London: Continuum, 2004

- Malcolm Bradbury: *The Novel Today*. Manchester: Manchester University Press, 1977.

- *Brewer's Dictionary of Phrase and Fable*. London: Brewer's, 2012.

- Jane Bussmann: *A Journey to the Dark Heart of Nameless Unspeakable Evil: Charities, Hollywood, Joseph Kony, and Other Abominations*. Santa Ana, CA: Nortia Press, 2014

- William Goldman: *Adventures in the Screen Trade*. London: Macdonald, 1984, c1983.

- Clive James: *Cultural Amnesia: Notes in the Margin of My Time*. London: Picador, 2007.

- Stephen King: *On Writing*. London: Hodder, 2012.

- David Lodge: *The Art of Fiction*. London: Penguin, 1992.

- Rob Long: *Conversations with My Agent*. London: Faber and Faber, 1996.

- Robert McKee: *Story: Substance, Structure, Style, and the Principles of Screenwriting*. London: Methuen, 1999.

- Caitlin Moran: *How to Be a Woman*. London: Ebury, 2012.

- Keith Waterhouse: *Billy Liar*. Harmondsworth: Penguin, 1974.

- Keith Waterhouse: *Waterhouse on Newspaper Style*. Brighton: Revel Barker Publishing, 2010.

## Appendix:

# THE JOHN GIELGUD UMBRELLA STORY

This story was told to me and several other people in a pub called The George after an edition of *Loose Ends*, by the much-missed writer, broadcaster and producer Ned Sherrin. I am justifying the inclusion of this story because a) it's a perfect example of how to tell a story b) it's a perfect example of how to tell a story within a story c) it is arguably good advice for any performer and d) I am very fond of it.

Sir John Gielgud was directing a play in the West End of London when one of the cast members paused while delivering a speech. 'Oh no,' said Sir John. 'That won't do at all. You must never pause when delivering a speech in the West End. I once paused while I was delivering the soliloquy from *Hamlet*, and as I did so, a voice from the circle said, "Oh you brute! You've come all over my umbrella!"'